KILL THE *Jerk*

Rob Shepherd

Trilogy Christian Publishers
A Wholly Owned Subsidiary of Trinity Broadcasting Network
2442 Michelle Drive
Tustin, CA 92780

For information, address Trilogy Christian Publishing
Rights Department, 2442 Michelle Drive, Tustin, Ca 92780.
Trilogy Christian Publishing/ TBN and colophon are trademarks of Trinity Broadcasting Network.

For information about special discounts for bulk purchases, please contact Trilogy Christian Publishing.

Manufactured in the United States of America

10 9 8 7 6 5 4 3 2 1

Library of Congress Cataloging-in-Publication Data is available.

ISBN 978-1-64088-662-9 (Print Book)
ISBN 978-1-64088-663-6 (ebook)

Kill the Jerk is dedicated to Monica, Reese, and Hayden. Out of everything I do, I love being your husband and dad the most. I love you with all my heart.

To Next Level Church, thank you for being full of awesome! We are better together. So many of the lessons in this book have been lived out with you. The church isn't a pastor, and it's not a building. The church is people, and together we get to change the world!

CONTENTS

THE COOKIE CREW

It's been said that authors are starving artists. Thankfully, I have a full-time job as a pastor. With that being said, self-publishing is expensive, and this book was financed with the help of the Cookie Crew. The Cookie Crew is an amazing group of people who bought my locally famous for-people-who-know-me chocolate chip cookies. There were many people who paid $10 for a dozen cookies. The following people purchased the $30 or more option, which in turn royally helped me raise the funds to publish this book. Thank you, Cookie Crew!

1. Marcia and Bob Shepherd
2. Laura Lowe
3. Karen Dempster
4. Kim and Ryan Windle
5. Mike and Yvonne Hysick
6. Ryan King
7. Kelvin and Kim Edwards
8. Jimmy and Amy Williams
9. Susan Fraser
10. Bobby Benitez
11. Corrigan and Leah Threlkeld
12. Lindsey Enzor
13. Mary Pinksaw
14. Dr. Bowler's Dental Office
15. Tabitha Childers
16. LaQuan Green
17. Matt and Ki Wilbur
18. Curt and Marilyn Thompson
19. Hope Carraway

20. Eric and Stacy Froyen
21. Donald and Ruth Peters
22. Leslie McClees
23. Stacey Smithley
24. Greg and Sabrina Michalov
25. Tim and Desiree Vaughn
26. Theresa Olmes
27. Jessica Kurtz
28. Hampton Roads Fellowship
29. Chantel Firman
30. Darrold and Margo Peters
31. Mike Manicone
32. Kelly Maloney
33. Garrett Williams
34. Deedee and Courtney Weaver
35. Ryan and Cyndy Somerset
36. Carole Hochoy
37. Jeanne Fiocca
38. Charlotte Marie Callins
39. Doug and Teresa Crowson
40. Gary and Mary Webb
41. Doug and Laurie Norton
42. Kim Lambright
43. Angela York
44. Ron Clark
45. Rob and JJ Bastian
46. Elizabeth Smith
47. Charlotte Dillow
48. Vince and Heather Seidnitzer
49. Mike and Linda McKelvey
50. Joe and Donna Blanchard
51. Andrew Turner
52. Kevin Wilkins
53. Tanner and Denice
54. Austin and Alexa Waggoner
55. Christina Triantafillou
56. Ashwin Singh
57. Ronald and Kristina Creech
58. Jason and Michelle Covington
59. Rob and Karen Self

INTRODUCTION

Why this book? I'm glad you asked. *Kill the Jerk* is written out of a desire to help people have healthy relationships. I have a heart for people to truly thrive relationally. I believe you can't do life alone, and yet many people are trying because they have been wounded by others. Relationships are difficult. Over half of all marriages end in divorce, since 1985 the number of Americans with no close friendships has tripled, and way too many people settle for unhealthy relationships because it seems that is all there is. Whether it's friendships, dating, marriage, neighbors, coworkers, or family, all relationships have a degree of difficulty. I want to help. I don't claim to know it all, and one book won't heal all relationships. My prayer is that this book will be used as a piece of the relational puzzle that leads to healthy connections.

This book started out with the title, "People Don't Come with Instructions." The idea was birthed after helping someone through pastoral counseling. After one session a person I was counseling said, "I wish there was a rule book for relationships. What I've learned in our time together is eye-opening, and I wish I would have learned it earlier." At that point I thought, *I'm going to write a book on the helpful principles I use to help myself and others have healthy relationships.* I spent a few weeks working on that book. I mapped out the chapters, wrote summaries of each chapter, and started collecting research. I even preached a sermon series at my church under that name. I was well on my way to writing "People Don't Come with Instructions" when I was hit with a problem. While working on the second chapter, I realized that jerks don't follow rules. That's one of the things that makes them a jerk. Jerks are driven by feelings, and when the feelings hit, their emotions trump any rules. That's one of the many things that are so frustrating about jerks. They are the ones who act as if the rules don't apply. So I started to wonder how I could help jerks have healthy relationships.

That thought started to capture me. Thus, a new book was born. Maybe one day I'll write a book about healthy rules for relationships, but before that book, this one had to be written. This isn't a book just for married people or dating people. It's not a book just for people in love. It's a book for anyone who has a relationship with another human or wants to. It's a book for friends, coworkers, neighbors, and especially anyone who spends time online. Jerks often feel courageous when they are sitting behind a computer screen or smartphone. This is a book for anyone who wants healthier relationships. I'll get to how to kill the jerk in chapter 1, but before that there are a few things I'd like to cover.

1. This a book based out of real-life principles that I have used and helped others use to have healthy relationships. It is not a psychological study of jerks. It's not an exhaustive resource for every jerk that exists. I use some psychology, but I also use a lot of Scripture. I take a practical look at how we can apply Scripture to have healthy relationships. It was suggested to me to make the book more appealing by removing the Scripture. As a pastor and Christian, that wasn't an option for me. You

do not have to be a Christian to read this book, but know that I am, and thus, Jesus is the model for in which I want to build healthy relationships.

2. Every chapter has a Big Idea. The Big Idea is a way to summarize the chapter in a memorable way. My hope was to write a book that people enjoy reading but at the same time it is helpful to people. The Big Idea is a way to take a nugget of info with you after you finish the chapter.
3. Every chapter has Win. The Win is the application of the chapter. As a person who reads books, I'm often frustrated with a lack of application. That is, at times I am not smart enough to know what my next step is. The Win is a potential next step. It doesn't have to be yours. My prayer is that God will use this book to do immeasurably more than I could ask or imagine. You may have a different win, and that's okay. Just know if you ever get to the end of a chapter and aren't sure what next step to take, I provide one.
4. There are questions at the end of each chapter. The questions can be used for individual or group study. Because this is a book about relationships, I think it will be utilized the most in groups. It can be read by individuals 100 percent; but if you have a friend, relative, coworker, spouse, or church small group that wants to work on having healthy relationships, ask them to read the book with you. If you have a church small group, book club, or Facebook group that would benefit from this book, then go through the questions together. The questions are designed to help each reader gain self-awareness and apply what he or she is learning.

5. If you like what you read, please remember that sharing is caring. Please share your positive experiences by writing a review online at a book distributor or sharing what you like on social media. If you hate what you read, please remember that the title of this book is *Boundaries* by Cloud and Townsend. I kid, I kid. *Boundaries* is an amazing book that has sold over two million copies. I figured if you hate this book and wrote a negative review about *Boundaries*, it wouldn't impact their book sales.

Now that we have covered all of that you are ready to dive in. Thank you for reading my book. I pray it's helpful and enjoyable for you. Now let's go kill the jerk!

CHAPTER 1

Kill the Jerk

I'm not a violent person. I am a pastor. I'm a pastor who is against killing people. So if you were looking for a book on how to Mafia style take out someone, then this isn't the book for you. Now you are asking, "What's the deal with the title?" Great question. I'm glad you asked it.

In the Scriptures Jesus often used hyperbole when he taught. For example, Jesus said, "And if your eye causes you to stumble, gouge it out and throw it away. It is better for you to enter life with one eye than to have two eyes and be thrown into the fire of hell" (Matt. 18:9).

I like the way the King James Version translates this verse. It uses the word *pluck* instead of *gouge*. It's still brutal but somehow seems more civilized. It's like plucking a gray hair, nose hairs, or any other unwanted body hair. Even the more gentle word choice of *pluck* is still an attention getter when it applies to your eyeballs. And Jesus said it! Jesus did say it, but we have zero examples of anyone in Jesus's day who heard him say this literally plucking their cornea out. Jesus often used strong language to get people's attention. He wasn't being literal. Neither am I.

Now you are thinking, *Oh, so this is just click bait to get people to buy your book!* I wouldn't use the phrase *click bait.* I did pick the title to grab people's attention, but I also really want people to kill the jerk. To understand what I mean let's define some words.

The word *kill* means a couple of different things according to the dictionary.

kill
/kil/
verb

1. Cause the death of (a person, animal, or other living thing)
   "Her father was killed in a car crash"
2. Put an end to or cause the failure or defeat of (something)
   "The committee voted to kill the project."

The second definition is more in line with what I'm writing about, so put away your weapons of mass destruction. In order to have healthy relationships, we must defeat, squash, vanquish, put an end to, or kill unhealthy practices. *Kill* is a violent word, and you cannot get around that. Sometimes strong language is needed to make a point. The truth is, there are some things we cannot compromise if we want to truly experience change. All relationships have issues, and some of those issues are so destructive we have to be bold in our strategy to overcome them. It won't be easy, but nothing worthwhile ever is. In order to find some progress, we cannot ignore the jerk, mildly shoo the jerk away, tickle fight the jerk, or just hope that the jerk goes away. We have to get serious about eliminating the jerk.

So now you are asking, "Who is the jerk?" First off, I really appreciate you asking so many good questions. Second off, the questions are good but this book is going to get long if you keep interjecting them. My last book is almost four hundred pages, and I'm trying to keep this one at two hundred pages. How about we save questions until the end? Third off, the jerk is probably not who you are thinking of. But first, some history.

The History of Jerk

The definition of *jerk* doesn't help us much because it is different than what most of us think about when we use the term. The original idea of a jerk is very different than what I think of when I think about that term. I think about someone who is rude, insensitive, angry, or selfishly puts their needs ahead of everyone else's. That's not what the definition of jerk is.

> jerk
> /jərk/
> noun
> informal
> a contemptibly obnoxious person
> Synonyms: fool, idiot, another word for a donkey named Jack (*pastoral edit*), halfwit, nincompoop, blockhead, buffoon, dunce, dolt, ignoramus.

Did you read the synonyms for jerk? Those are some pretty good insults. I personally like the word *halfwit.* Can you be a whole-whit? Or if you are average, are you just a whit? I digress. The definition of jerk defines someone that I would call an idiot, not someone who is rude.

I first discovered this difference by watching movies from the eighties. In the classic film *Goonies* one of my favorite characters is Chunk. He's hilarious. He is not mean or rude in any way, and yet when the other Goonies see him for the first time in the film, they describe him by saying, "Jerk alert." This same type of usage is found in other films like *Back to the Future* and most notably in the film called *The Jerk*. I'm not sure exactly when, but some time between the end of the eighties and now, the word *jerk* stopped meaning someone who is dumb and started to describe someone who was rude. That is the cultural understanding of jerk. For this book the cultural understanding of jerk is what I'm going for.

A jerk is someone who

- doesn't respect others opinions or beliefs,
- is rude,
- has little to no regard for others, and
- is selfish.

Kids Are Jerks

Everyone knows someone who is a jerk. It only takes spending thirty seconds on social media, driving in heavy traffic where there is a lane closure, or having a kid to find a jerk. That's right. I wrote it. Kids are jerks. Let me rephrase that, kids can be jerks. No one has to teach a child how to be a jerk. I promise I'm going somewhere with this. Stick with me. Kids are born with a natural jerk inside of them. I love my kids, and for the most part both of them are kind. They are well-behaved, nice, and I have a lot of fun with them. One of my greatest joys in life is being their dad. As great as my kids are, it doesn't take much for their inner jerk to come out. Especially with each other. Put two siblings together in the back seat of a car, and you will see just how jerk like kids can be. It is not uncommon for my kids to forget their manners and push in front of the other to get something, believe the worst (*He did it on purpose!*), and demand that they get what they want. I've never had to teach my kids how to be selfish, lie, or declare, "*Mine!*"

I stand by my statement. Kids can be jerks. I know, I was a kid once. One time when we went to get family pictures I became unhappy about who knows what. The following picture is the result.

I was a pretty happy kid. Based on a few of our family pics, I was a jerk. I remember this pic. I remember being told to smile for the camera. I didn't think through how my actions impacted my family. I just reacted. I didn't want to take the picture. I didn't think through the fact that my parents paid for this. I didn't think through this picture would be a forever reminder of my bad attitude. I feel bad for my parents. To help make up for this, my siblings got together to recreate this pic as adults.

Since I was a jerk of a kid, it only makes sense that I would pass on some jerk qualities to my kids. If you've ever been around kids, you know they are like having a blender set to high and there is no lid. The battles they pick to fight are silly, selfish, and exhausting. Parenting is not for the faint of heart. I've heard it said that parenting is as easy as a walk in the park...Jurassic Park.

Now you are thinking, *Rob, you are being mean to your kids.* Loosen up! Listen, singles. Stop judging me. I'm assuming the judgment is coming from those without kids. Every parent knows what I've written is true. Plus, I've already covered this. Let's keep questions until the end. Also, I would never call my kids a jerk to their faces. I wouldn't want to be a jerk. I kid, I kid. To answer your thought, I'm giving examples of kids being jerks for a specific reason.

Just Tell Me Who the Jerk Is Already!

You are the jerk. Don't get mad! If you are thinking, *I'm not a jerk, you are,* then you are partially right. You are the jerk. I'm also the jerk. All humans have an inner jerk. We don't like to think about our inner jerk. We often hide him, ignore him, or rationalize him away; but he's there. We are often blinded to our inner jerk. At times he is so loud we see him clearly, but other times he comes out and we don't even realize he's in control. The jerk is easier to see in others than it is in ourselves. I'm convinced that if we truly saw our inner jerk, there would be a lot more kindness in the world. There are specific reasons we are blind to our own jerk, and I'll cover those in this book. There are also times where we feel justified to be a jerk, and I'll cover that as well. We cannot escape all the jerks out there. We will deal with others who are jerks on a regular basis, and we cannot kill them. We also cannot always avoid them. We cannot control other jerks, so we should work on controlling the inner jerk. By controlling, I mean killing him. In order to see new life something has to die. It's difficult to die to oneself, but it brings new life. In order to experience new life, Jesus had to die. I know you have a lot of excuses and rationalizations as to why you can be a jerk, but in order to receive new life, he must die.

In this book I'm going to do everything I can to help you kill the inner jerk. As parents we do our best to help our kids learn to not be jerks. Every adult was once a kid, and depending on your home-life, you may or may not have had your natural jerk tendencies reprimanded. Through interaction with others, we often learn what jerk-like behaviors exist inside of us. As kids grow into adults, they don't naturally eliminate the jerk inside. For examples of this visit a middle school. As we become adults we learn to hide the jerk, disguise the jerk, and then turn a blind eye to our own personal jerkiness. Kids at least are honest. As adults we try to be on our best behavior around people we don't know well. Way too often we only unleash the jerk toward those that are closest to us. How messed up is that?

I have found that a lot of adults are older versions of toddlers. They may use different words, but it doesn't take much for them to have a meltdown. And meltdowns are usually about not getting their way, being hungry, and or tired. If you want to see someone's inner jerk, watch them when they don't get their way.

One of the main issues with being a jerk is it's easy to spot in others but incredibly difficult to see in ourselves. There are some people who embrace their inner jerk. These are people who are rude and know it. I almost respect someone who embraces their jerk. Even still, I think if someone who has embraced their jerk could watch themselves be a jerk on camera they'd be embarrassed and try to change their ways. As a recovering people pleaser, I hide my inner jerk from everyone except for those I love the most. Jerk! Some people are not self-aware enough to see their inner jerk. This person isn't intentionally trying to be a jerk; but because they don't know how others perceive them, they often offend, wound, or hurt others without even knowing it.

Many people will say, "Well, that's just how I am, take it or leave it!" That's a fair statement when it comes to knowing your weaknesses, but at some point, it becomes an excuse. As a Christian it's your responsibility to figure out how your inner jerk is negatively impacting other people and the ones you love. If you truly believe that you don't have to change anything about yourself, especially the worst parts, then I hope you allow others to keep the same standard. It's not fair to get upset at someone else for being a jerk if your response is, "That's just how I am." If you do, please make sure the next time someone cuts in front of you in traffic, gives you bad service at a restaurant, takes something that is yours, or makes you angry in any way, that you smile and say, "That's just who they are. They can't help it." If everyone holds on to "That's just how I am," then the world will never get better. At some point someone has to stand up, be an adult, and declare, "In order to change the world, I've got to start with myself."

The vast majority of people naturally view themselves through rose-colored lenses. That is, we tend to turn a blind eye to the jerk that lives inside of us. I don't know anyone who when meeting new people leads with, "Let me tell you about all my flaws." Having a jerk inside of you doesn't mean you are 100 percent a jerk. It does mean that you have the potential to be a jerk. At times the jerk is easy to ignore because we typically believe that if our good outweighs our bad, then we are good to go. That's a common thought, but it's not true. We don't keep track of all the little offenses we do, and we over evaluate the good that we do. At times we give ourselves credit for thinking about doing something nice. That's jacked up. Finding your inner jerk is not about competing with other jerks. It's about finding the jerk in you and dealing with him.

It's sad that so often we give our best to those who know us the least. Following Jesus is more than going to church and following a few rules. Jesus is more than a Sunday thing. Jesus wants to save us. All of us. Including the inner jerk. In fact, it is impossible to follow Jesus and not become great at loving people. If you love Jesus but don't like people, something is off. If you love Jesus but don't want to be great at relationships, something is off. Loving Jesus and loving people are connected.

Until we address the jerk that lives inside of us, we will not give our best to those we love the most. Until we address the inner jerk, we will see the flaws of others and use them as a way to distract us from improving ourselves. In fact, until we address our inner jerk, we will rationalize his behavior. I don't know about you, but I want to love the people I'm closest to the best. I am often kinder to strangers or new friends than I am to those I love the most. Rarely, when driving with friends do I let my anger at other drivers come out. When it's just me and my wife, I let the Christian curse words fly. You know, words like "What the hey!" or "Jack hole" or "Shut the front door!" or "Mother Fiddlesticks!" You know when you clean up the word but don't address the heart behind the word that is a Christian curse word. I'm a work in progress. Jerk!

What makes it even more difficult is the fact that when the jerk does come out, we often feel justified. The inner jerk comes out when we feel wronged, hurt, or left out. The jerk turns a blind eye to one's own actions because they are justified based on what the other person has done. It's difficult to see what a jerk I am as long as I focus on other people's issues. We are around our families the most, so they see the jerk inside of us the most. Because the jerk is hidden inside of me, I often don't think about him. I don't think about him until after he has roared his ugly face and unleashed on someone I love. At times I don't see the jerk when he comes out because I'm so focused on what the other person has done to me. It's like we feel it's okay to be a jerk if someone has wronged us. The jerk feels justified when someone hurts us, doesn't meet our expectations, offends us, or doesn't get what he wants. You can learn a lot about a person when they don't get their way. You can learn a lot about yourself when you don't get your way. That's when the jerk comes out, and when he does show his ugly face, he will be focused on the issues of others. We will feel justified and want to get back at the person who wronged us, hurt us, or didn't give us what we want. The problem is that's not what Jesus taught! Jesus taught to love our enemies, turn the other cheek, and pray for those who persecute us. When the jerk comes out, I rarely see him because he feels justified. It's not until after I unleash the jerk on someone that I realize I was the one in the wrong. You can be right and still handle it wrong. This is why we have to kill the jerk. That is we have to address the jerk that lives inside of us. I have to kill my inner jerk, and I'm encouraging you to kill the one that lives inside of you. Just a warning, that joker isn't easy to kill and often comes back from the dead. The jerk is not easy to deal with, but until we do we will never see progress in our relationships. We will have facade relationships with people we barely know. Meanwhile, those that we know the best will often get our worst. We will have picture-perfect relationships for social media all the while our time with the people we love will be broken, rotten, or dysfunctional. This shouldn't be! The people we are closest to should get our best, not our worst. Whether your inner jerk comes out occasionally or daily, true life change won't happen until you address the jerk.

The Honeymoon Effect

When you first meet someone, especially someone you like, the natural tendency is to be on your best behavior. We know how judgmental people can be, so we intentionally try to not do anything that would cause a new relationship to judge us harshly. We do not like to feel rejected, so when we meet someone new that we want to impress, we bring out our best. It's not necessarily an act. It's a decision to show off the best parts about you in order to win someone over. It's the same reason that a lot of us clean our house for company, but let the mess build when it's just our family. There is something inside of us that wants love but is afraid that only our best is truly lovable. This is ingrained in us. This is why, often kids are better behaved for babysitters or teachers than they are for their own parents. It means a kid feels safe around the parent in order to be their true selves. Around someone new, especially someone we look to impress, we put on a little show. We are the best version of ourselves. We give our best at the beginning and subconsciously hide the not so glamorous. This time of being on your best behavior is known as the honeymoon period. It's not just for marriages. We experience this with new jobs, friendships, and churches. It's during this period that we hide the inner jerk. We give our best and hide the areas that need some work. Whether it's being more romantic, showing up to work on time, or showing initiative to hang out, the honeymoon period is an intentional decision to bring our best. We naturally do this because internally we are afraid to lose this new relationship. We don't want to be rejected, so we naturally bring our best in hopes that we will be accepted. This doesn't last for long.

The honeymoon period lasts on average two years. It could be shorter or longer, but at some point from the start of a relationship to around the second-year mark the honeymoon period ends. This doesn't mean that you instantly become a jerk. If that was the case, this would be easier to fix. Instead the honeymoon period sneakily ends. We often don't see it coming, and it can take years to realize it's ended. The honeymoon period ends when we no longer fear the other person is going to leave. For example, in dating a guy most likely won't pass gas out loud on the first date. At least

I hope not. You can tell when the honeymoon period has ended when he is no longer afraid to let one rip in front of the woman of his dreams. Not only that, but often it comes in the form of a Dutch oven (pulling the blankets over your spouse's head after you fart to trap her in there). Jerk!

It's not just dating or romance. The same thing happens in friendship, at work, and at church. Not literally the same thing as farting in front of people, but you get the point. There is a time where we no longer feel afraid, and when that happens we stop trying to impress the people closest to us. At this point we naturally take the person we love for granted. When we are no longer afraid that the other person is going to leave, our true self comes out and it's often ugly. This is where we forget anniversaries, stop being polite, say what we really feel, and/or prioritize other things because we know the person will still be there. How messed up is that? That is the inner jerk.

We are often the most defensive with those we love the most. We naturally believe the worst. We snap at them quickly. We encourage them the least and point out their flaws the most. Even worse is the fact that once the honeymoon period ends, we tend to neglect the people that are closest to us.

The people we are closest to are the ones we take the most for granted.

At a job it's after the honeymoon period that people start slacking. The temptation is to not put in as much work as we did on day one. We may cut corners, or we may not show the same enthusiasm for the job. When we have job security, we naturally tend to slack off. It's the same thing in relationships. The reason absence makes the heart grow fonder is because it is in absence that we realize what we really care about. Day-to-day interaction leads to taking people for granted. This is why most married couples don't schedule regular date nights. It's why most people don't have close friendships. Unless we are intentional, we will truly not know what we have until it's gone. Unless we are intentional, even good marriages will become more roommates than soul mates, jobs will become necessary evils, and friends will be neglected. You have a choice to make. You can wait until someone you love moves or dies to realize how much you appreciate them, or you can do the hard work to love the people closest to you the most.

Way too often couples neglect one another until one of them cannot take it any longer. At this point one of them says the words, "I want a divorce." And at this time, very often the other person reacts by overcompensating in kindness. The romance picks up, the kindness picks up, and the love goes back to how it was during the early days of the honeymoon phase. The issue is, the person who asked for the divorce thinks, *They didn't really change. He only is doing this to win me back. As soon as I commit, he will go back to his old ways.* I hear this type of thing often with couples. When the fear of the other person is reintroduced, the honeymoon phase comes back in full force. Humans do this naturally, but when it's done in response to brokenness, the person on the other side questions the genuineness of the change. Once someone feels the other person is only being nice because of the threat of divorce, the relationship is difficult to work on. Every time the other person does something nice, it is being judged through the lens of inauthenticity. This doesn't just happen in married couples. It can also happen in jobs, with kids, and friendships. A person unintentionally neglects someone they truly care about, and thus the neglected person ends up leaving. At this point it's a wake-up call, but often it is too late. This is why way too often we do not realize what we have until it's gone. Our brains are wired to take for granted the ones we love the most. Jerk!

This is why humans wait until funerals, retirements, or when someone is moving to share how they really feel. At that point it's often too late. Spouses should be the biggest cheerleaders of one another; instead, they are often the harshest critic. Friends should be the best at supporting one another, and yet it's often easy to neglect spending time with friends. The people we know should be encouraged the most from us, but it's rarely that way. Familiarity breeds neglect. Think about it with your house or the place you stay. When it was new, you most likely appreciated it more and took care of it. After a while you become familiar with it. It doesn't mean you don't appreciate it, but you have now become used to the stains on the carpet or other imperfections of the house. We do the same thing with relationships.

Why is it that the people closest to us get the worst version of ourselves? I've wondered this when it comes to how I interact with my parents. I'm a nice guy. I don't think very many people would ever call me a jerk. But my fuse is short with my parents. They were great parents, and I reward them by snapping at them whenever they get on my nerves. Jerk. I'm a work in progress. I don't always get this right, but I have come a long way. I've been intentionally applying what I've written about in this book, and I can say I've seen great improvement. My natural jerk comes out the strongest around the people I know love me the most. I know it's because I know they will love me unconditionally, but I don't want to take that for granted. I'm better today than ever, and I hope to continue to grow. I want those closest to me to get my best, not my worst.

I'm convinced that true change doesn't happen until we deal with our jerk. For some reason we don't think the jerk is our real self, but it is. The real self comes out when you feel comfortable. That real self is a reflection of the condition of your heart.

I cannot even count the number of times I've counseled couples who were on the brink of divorce. The reason? They fell out of love. Why did they fall out of love? Because one or both stopped doing whatever it took to keep the person they were married to.

It's crazy how people will prioritize their jobs over their kids because they feel a child's love is unconditional only to wake up and have their now teenager want nothing to do with them. Why are we so broken that we bring out our best to win someone over, but then once we win them, they often get our worst?

Here's my goal—kill the jerk. That is, I want the people closest to me to get my best and not my worst.

Everyone wants healthy relationships, but few people are willing to do the work necessary to have healthy relationships. If you want healthy relationships, it will take some intentional work. Nothing great is sustained accidentally. That takes us to the big idea of this chapter.

Big Idea: In order to have healthy relationships we must identify the inner jerk and crucify him.

Then Jesus said to his disciples, "Whoever wants to be my disciple must deny themselves and take up their cross and follow me. For whoever wants to save their life will lose it, but whoever loses their life for me will find it" (Matt. 16:24–25).

That's what this book is about. It's about helping you discover the jerk inside and crucifying him. Crucifixion was a brutal way to die. Jesus knew that in order for us to have life something had to die. That something was Him. When we die to ourselves and follow Jesus, we come to life. Until the old things die, we will not see the fruit of new things. Until the old ways of treating people changes, we won't see the fruit of healthy relationships. Think about your relationships. From childhood until now how many of them are healthy, not just enduring or okay? How many of them are thriving? Many people have spent their entire lives in broken relationships, and I want to help that. That's what this book is about. It's about you learning to love others the way God loves you. It's about learning to not neglect the people you truly care about. It's about you not taking for granted those you love the most. It's about truly having healthy relationships. It's about giving our best to the ones we love the most. It's about having a private life that matches the public life. We cannot do that until we deal with the jerk that lives inside. Who is with me? I'll see you in chapter 2.

The Win for this chapter: Commit to finish reading this book.

Questions for Further Reflection

1. On a scale of 1 to 10 (1 being no sign of a jerk and 10 being full-blown jerk), what number would you give yourself?
2. Why didn't you go lower in your number?
3. Imagine you were less of a jerk. What would the positive outcomes be?
4. Why are those positive outcomes important to you?
5. What is the next step you should take to kill the jerk inside you?

CHAPTER 2

Treat Others How You Want to Be Treated

It seems that for every controversial issue there are two responses:

1. Full acceptance
2. Full rejection

When we disagree with someone and we do not want to be a jerk, we think we have to fully accept the person. When we cannot wrap our minds around accepting them, we jump to the other extreme of rejecting them completely. You often see the inner jerk come out during disagreements online. It's like we don't know how to respond other than to fully accept or fully reject someone. I believe there should be a third option.

In the Roman government the common way to treat others was based on *liberalitas. Liberalitas* is the Latin word that means, "You give in order to get something in return." The common thought in the Roman society was to bless those that could benefit you and disregard those who cannot. So if someone had something you wanted, then you found a way to bless them. If they didn't, then they were expendable. Historic jerks!

In many ways I feel America has adopted *liberalitas*. When we agree with someone, we bless them. When we disagree with them, we destroy them. There is very little room for people who cannot benefit our own agenda, ideas, or way of living. Modern jerks!

Full acceptance or full rejection.

As an American I've often wondered how Jesus was a "friend to sinners." There is no way He agreed with everything they did, but at the same time He did not reject them. Jesus ate meals with the sinners that the religious elite rejected. Jesus was a friend to sinners, but He did not approve of their sin. Thus, we have a third option. The third option helps direct our feelings.

Most of the time we base relationships on how we feel. The problem is feelings are futile. Feelings change. Have you ever jumped into a relationship with someone you thought was a good friend only to have your feelings change? Have you ever started dating someone only to realize that your feelings changed? I can tell you there were some girls that I thought I was in love with and now when I look back I thank God He didn't answer those prayers. How many times have you looked back at old photos and saw how your feelings changed about fashion? At one point in my history, I wore a lot of silk shirts. Why? I don't have a fat clue, but the pictures are buried deep down where no one will find them. Thank God social media did not exist when I was a sophomore in high school. There have been times my feelings led me to eat Taco Bell only to regret that decision once it's been digested. Taco Bell is the best-tasting laxative. I've regretted my decision to eat it on road trips, and even vowed to never eat it again after one uncomfortable meeting at the church. Feelings lie! How many times have you committed to something only to have your feelings change the day of the event? Feelings are not reliable. Feelings go up and down. Based on the honeymoon phase, feelings will change once the relationship no longer feels new.

Feelings can be difficult, and because you have feelings, at times you are difficult.

We often can't see what a jerk we are, er, how difficult we truly are because we live our life by our feelings. When feelings direct your behavior, survival is your main concern. So if you are feeling angry, you'll snap at someone. If you are feeling sad, you may pull away from someone. If you are feeling overwhelmed, you may ignore someone. What may feel natural to you may also be the thing that hinders having healthy relationships. Feelings are not right or wrong, but what we do with feelings can be. Feelings can be strong, and we shouldn't feel ashamed about having feelings. At the same time we need to be careful to not let our feelings control us. Feelings are important, but they shouldn't be controlling. When we have a feeling, we should do something about it. Ignoring a feeling is not healthy. Allowing it to control us is just as unhealthy. I believe there is another way. It's not easy, but it's more healthy.

Dr. Alexandra Solomon offers some great insight into this by saying, "The next time you're having a hard time, try this: Instead of saying to yourself, 'I am not okay,' say to yourself, 'I am feeling deeply.' Notice what shifts inside you." This is a way to try and control your feelings instead of letting them control you. It's not healthy to bury feelings. It's also not helpful to allow feelings to cause us to erupt.

Emotions without action is constipation. That is, if you do not deal with emotions in a healthy way, they will hurt you and ultimately your relationships. Holding emotions inside, denying emotions, and burying emotions only delays the response. When the delayed response finally does come out, it's worse because it's had time to simmer.

Feelings can be big and at times scary to deal with. At the same time having strong feelings does not mean that we allow them to control us, hurt others, or be an excuse for bad behavior. The jerk inside lives on feelings. The jerk inside will say, "If they hurt me, unleash hell on them." The jerk inside will say, "React quickly to what has just happened to you." The jerk inside does not have your best interest in mind. Your best interest is to have healthy relationships. The jerk inside will fight to get what you want, even if it hurts others. I think some of us know this, and this is why we bury feelings deep down. We don't want to face them because we are afraid of what our inner jerk will do.

Jesus wants to redeem our feelings. As Pastor Mark Batterson says, "It's way easier to act like a Christian than to react like one." It's easier to learn how to pretend to have a great life, amazing relationships, and true happiness than it is to actually have it. In order to have healthy relationships, we have to allow Jesus to save our minds in addition to our hearts. If you are a Christian, then at some point you allowed Jesus to save your soul but Jesus said that the greatest command was to love God with all our heart, soul, and mind. That's our entire being including our feelings. Jesus wants us to honor him with our feelings. Feelings aren't necessarily wrong, but uncontrolled feelings lead to all sorts of issues. For those of us that are parents we know this. We often tell our kids to control themselves when their feelings become big, but then we turn around and allow our feelings to control us. There is nothing wrong with having feelings. The issue is when our feelings have us.

What if, instead of allowing our feelings to dictate how we treat other people, we live by a conviction that supersedes our feelings? That is, we lived by a principle that helped direct our strong feelings. That leads to what this chapter is all about and to the third option.

Big Idea: Treat others how you want to be treated, not how you are feeling.

I want to show you this in Scripture. This was a common teaching of Jesus. He repeated it multiple times.

> Do to others as you would have them do
> to you. (Luke 6:31, NIV)

Let's stop there for a second. This is known as the golden rule. It's one of Jesus's most famous teachings. This teaching is not unique to Jesus. In fact, a version of this was very popular in Jesus's day. Rabbi Hillel was teaching during the time of Jesus's childhood. He is famous for saying, "What is hateful to yourself, do not do to other people." Now this is similar to Jesus's teaching, but it's the negative form. Whatever you hate yourself, don't do to others.

I hate lima beans. Hate them! It goes back to a time from my childhood. My mom made them for dinner, and I was being a jerk of a kid. I refused to eat them. I wasn't alone in this boycott. My sister and brother were with me in this decision to picket the lima beans. That was until my mom said, "If you do not eat your lima beans, then you do not get dessert." My sister couldn't handle this and crossed the picket line. She caved and shoveled the lima beans down her throat.

She finished and declared, "I get dessert!" That was followed up with power puking said lima beans back onto her plate. That moment scarred me. It was like a scene out of the movie *The Exorcist*. The only logical reaction to this is to write off lima beans for all eternity. To this day I don't eat lima beans. So based on Rabi Hillel's teaching, because I hate lima beans, I should never serve lima beans. The problem is that my wife, Monica, loves lima beans. The negative form of the golden rule falls short of truly serving others because it's based on what you hate or don't want to happen to you.

The negative version of the golden rule appears in many world religions.

- Thales: Avoid doing what you would blame others for doing.
  (first philosopher in the Greek tradition)
- Confucius: Do not do to others that which we do not want them to do to us.
  (Chinese teacher and philosopher 500 BC)
- Hinduism: This is the sum of duty; do naught onto others what you would not have them do unto you.
- Buddhism: Hurt not others with that which pains yourself.
- Judaism: That which is hateful to you, do not do to your fellow. That is the whole Torah; the rest is the explanation; go and learn.
  (Old Testament of the Bible)

Some have even called this the silver rule. It's still a good teaching. Jesus does something amazing with the silver rule! He takes a very popular teaching and flips the script on it. Jesus turns the negative form into a positive form.

Do to others as you would have them do to you. This is a powerful tweak. I hate lima beans, but because I love Monica, I should make it rain lima beans on her dinner plate. I should treat her the way I want to be treated. Why? Because I'm called to do to others as I would have them do to me. Most of us wait for our feelings to dictate how we treat others. That's passive. The golden rule isn't passive like the negative form. This is active.

When you get offended, isn't it because someone did something that you would never do? We think, *I can't believe they didn't invite me. I would never do that to them!* Or we think, *I can't believe she ignored me, I would never do that to her!* Or *I can't believe he lied to me, I would never do that to him!* I think we are pretty good at living by the silver rule. I don't do to others what I don't want done to me. We often judge others based on the rules in which we live. If we wouldn't do it, we can't fathom why someone else would. Jesus's teaching is much more difficult.

So when someone mistreats you, think about how you would want to be treated if you mistreated someone else? Why is this so important? It's important because nothing reveals your affection for Jesus like how you treat other people. The issue with the jerk is that he has a double standard. When you do something wrong, you want others to treat you with grace and mercy. When we make a mistake, we want grace. But when someone makes a mistake against us, we want vengeance. When someone does something wrong to you, the jerk comes out and wants them to hurt like you are hurting.

You have made mistakes. You have hurt someone in your life. You have dropped the ball at some point. Think about the biggest mistake you've ever made. When you got caught or had to come clean or were faced with apologizing for your mistake, how did you want the people to treat you?

Humans have difficulty forgiving someone else until we are that someone else. Often when we make a mistake we cannot fathom why the other person won't simply forgive us. Then when we get hurt we can't fathom how we can forgive the other person. Do you see how that's broken?

Christians should react like Jesus. If I were to form an opinion about Christians on the reactions I see on the Internet, it would not represent Jesus well. I believe if you asked most Christians what shapes their worldview, they would say, "The Bible." What we say and what we do should match. Don't let your emotions override your theology! If following Jesus shapes your life, it also shapes your reactions. It's easy to say things; it's much more difficult to live them out. It's like this restaurant in my area that is named "No. 1 Chinese Restaurant." That's the name. Why is it number one? The parking lot is almost always empty. I don't know anyone that goes there. They can say they are number one, but if they aren't the leading seller of Chinese food, then what they say doesn't matter. When asked about what their worldview is, many Christians might say "The Bible" but spend way more time being shaped by news media, culture, or their feelings than Scripture.

Nothing will reveal your worldview more than anger. When we get angry, it's important to ask, "How should I respond?" If your worldview is based on Jesus's teachings, you will hear, "Treat others like you want to be treated." When we get angry, the jerk comes out and becomes laser focused on the other person. When we feel hurt, offended, or wronged, we lose track of our own actions and can only see the person causing us discomfort. To kill the jerk we must take a second to ask, "How should I respond?" Look at what Jesus says next. It's one of those verses that we need to take some time to think about. I like to say, "Put this in your pipe and smoke it." If that offends you, then put this on your buffet and spend a lot of time chewing on it. If that offends you, then remember to treat me like you want to be treated not how you are feeling. Jesus goes on to say,

> If you love those who love you, what credit is that to you? Even sinners love those who love them. And if you do good to those who are good to you, what credit is that to you? Even sinners do that. And if you lend to those from whom you expect repayment, what credit is that to you? Even sinners lend to sinners, expecting to be repaid in full. (Luke 6:32–34)

Jesus is calling His followers to a higher standard. Sure, it's difficult. Sure, we are going to get it wrong. I'm afraid way too many Christians aren't even wrestling with this. We've adopted the world's standards and have forgotten that we represent Jesus. If you want to make a difference in the world, you have to be different. To only love the ones that love us is natural, but the God we serve is supernatural. He's called us to a higher standard. He's called us to love those that don't benefit us. I love the way the Message paraphrase communicates this verse:

> Here is a simple rule of thumb for behavior: Ask yourself what you want people to do for you; then grab the initiative and do it for them! If you only love the lovable, do you expect a pat on the back? Run-of-the-mill sinners do that. If you only help those who help you, do you expect

> a medal? Garden-variety sinners do that. If you only give for what you hope to get out of it, do you think that's charity? The stingiest of pawnbrokers does that. (Luke 6:32–34, The Message)

Grab the initiative. Do for others what you would want them to do for you. If you only give for what you hope to get out of it, that's selfish. Selfishness may get us what we want temporarily, but it leaves us feeling empty for the long run. Become the kind of friend you want to have. Become the type of employee you would want to have if you were the boss. Become the type of person you'd like to marry. The Message goes on to say,

> I tell you, love your enemies. Help and give without expecting a return. You'll never—I promise—regret it. Live out this God-created identity the way our Father lives toward us, generously and graciously, even when we're at our worst. Our Father is kind; you be kind.
>
> Don't pick on people, jump on their failures, criticize their faults—unless, of course, you want the same treatment. Don't condemn those who are down; that hardness can boomerang. Be easy on people; you'll find life a lot easier. Give away your life; you'll find life given back, but not merely given back—given back with bonus and blessing. Giving, not getting, is the way. Generosity begets generosity. (Luke 6:35–38, The Message)

It's so easy to see others' faults and failures. The jerk can't see himself as long as he is focusing on others' failures. Be easy on people, and you'll find life a lot easier. We get so frustrated with people when they live life differently than we do. It's easy to get frustrated with those that we love when they don't act like we do. It's in those moments that we need to ask, "If I was wrong, how would I want them to treat me?"

The story goes, Joe forgot his wedding anniversary. His wife, Susan, was mad. In a rage she demanded, "Tomorrow morning, I expect to find a gift in the driveway that goes from 0 to 200 in 6 seconds." She then emphatically added, "And it better be there!" The next morning when his wife woke up, she looked out the window to find a box gift wrapped in the middle of the driveway. She opened it and found a brand-new bathroom scale.

Get it? That's funny, but not funny. That is often how we treat others. When we want something, we demand it. When we don't get what we think we deserve, the inner jerk comes rearing his head and lets the other person have it. We cannot demand that others love us. We cannot nag others into loving us. We shouldn't guilt others into loving us. We can take the initiative and help others see how love is supposed to be. Jesus said,

> But love your enemies, do good to them, and lend to them without expecting to get anything back. Then your reward will be great, and you will be children of the Most High, because he is kind to the ungrateful and wicked. Be merciful, just as your Father is merciful. (Luke 6:35–36)

This is a radical teaching! When someone you love is having an off day, think about how you would want to be treated if you had an off day. If your boss is being unreasonable, think about how you would want to be treated when you were unreasonable. Whether it's feeling left out, interacting with someone with different political views, or catching someone acting like a jerk, it's crucial to remember how you would want to be treated if roles were reversed. Some people are jerks! You are some people. Since you've been a jerk, it should help you understand how you should respond to current jerks in your life.

Jesus didn't feel like dying on a cross for you, but He did. Jesus didn't feel like suffering for you, but He did! Jesus treated us how He wants to be treated, not how He was feeling. Christians are called to follow Jesus's example. We are called to follow His example more than we follow our feelings.

With controversial topics people tend to fully accept or fully reject. The third option presented by Jesus is to "Do to others as you would have them do to you." Translation: even when someone is wrong, treat them the way you would want to be treated if you were wrong. I don't have to fully accept or reject. I can understand where others are coming from and then respond in the way I would want if the roles were reversed. I may not feel like being kind to someone, but I can remember how I wish others treated me when I was a jerk.

I believe this is important in helping us understand love. Often when people talk about love it's in black-and-white terms. We have a difficult time loving those we disagree with. It's easy to either dismiss those we disagree with, or if we really love them, we change our theology to accept what we once viewed as wrong. Love does not mean you accept everything about everyone. Love does not mean that you agree with everything someone does. We are called to love people, and that's not a conditional calling. We are called to love others deeply even when we disagree with them. We do not have to change our convictions or views of Scripture in order to love others. We do have to change the way we treat others. When we disagree, we love by treating others how we would want to be treated.

This isn't just wishful thinking or pie-in-the-sky beliefs. Treating others how you want to be treated has the potential to change others. The following is a recreation of a Facebook conversation. I changed a few details and names to try and protect those involved, but the words are an accurate presentation of what happened.

In that real-life example it would have been easy to escalate the drama. I was so proud of John and many of the others in the comments. When we react based on our emotions, we escalate the problem instead of solving it. This is the way of Jesus. What was amazing to watch is how Ace changed his tone. It didn't mean he changed his opinion. Most likely he still disagrees with John, but he was wrong in his response. John was tempted to blast back at Ace. He wrote and then deleted multiple replies. I'm so proud of him for doing that. If John would have allowed his feelings to win, he would have reacted and in turn added fuel to the fire. I absolutely love that this interaction ended in forgiveness and not bitterness. I love that it ended with reconciliation. That's the way of Jesus.

Our culture has believed in the lie that in order to love someone you must agree with everything they believe or do. That is not true. If that's the case, Jesus would have never loved us. You can love someone even when you disagree with them. Showing someone kindness and love doesn't mean you approve of everything they do. This is why it's so important to remember if you were in the wrong, how would you want others to treat you? I know there are lots of jerks out there. You cannot control them. You can, on a good day, control yourself. With the help of Jesus, we can become the type of people that love those that don't love us back. We can become the type of people that love jerks but at the same time not allowing the jerks to wound us. We can learn to treat others the way we want to be treated and not how we are feeling. The way to do that is found in the next chapter. Until then, here are some questions for further reflection.

The Win for this chapter: Treat others like you want to be treated, not how you are feeling. When you are feeling big emotions, identify them. Take a deep breath, and say out loud, "I'm feeling deeply."

Questions for Further Reflection

1. When it comes to your feelings are you more of a feeler or more of a logical thinker?
2. There are lots of things we do not want to do, but we do it anyway. What are some things you don't feel like doing, but because of discipline, you do them?
3. Ultimately Christians are called to treat others like Jesus has treated us, not how we are feeling. Is this an easy or difficult thing for you to do? Why?
4. Imagine if Jesus didn't treat you the way He wanted to be treated. Imagine if instead of giving up His life on the cross, He gave you what you deserve. Instead, Jesus brings peace to our calamity, joy to our sorrow, light to our darkness, etc. Write out the specific ways Jesus has loved you through difficult seasons of your life.
5. Based on this chapter, what is the one thing you are going to take away?

CHAPTER 3

The Antidote to the Jerk

Big Idea: Empathy is the antidote to the inner jerk.

I hope you are still chewing on the last chapter. I get that it's not easy to love others that don't love us. I am too well aware of having emotions control me. It's impossible to treat others how we want to be treated when we are focused on ourselves. Sometimes our pain or hurt is so deep that it's all we can see. We need something to help us get our eyes off ourselves. If left unchecked, strong emotions have a way of destroying us from the inside out. When this happens, the jerk will come out regularly and we won't even notice it. Our hurt will blind us to our own actions. Because we are born selfish, when we feel pain we naturally turn inward.

If selfishness is the disease, then empathy is the antidote for the inner jerk. In order to treat others like I want to be treated, I must put myself in their shoes. That's empathy. Empathy is the ability to understand the feelings of others. Empathy doesn't mean that you agree with everything another person believes or does. Empathy means you try to understand what another person is going through. So often the inner jerk comes out and focuses on how we are feeling. When that happens, we unleash the kraken of an attitude. We are so focused on how others make us feel that we forget how our actions can make others feel. We justify ugly behavior because we can only see the other person's wrongdoing. Don't let someone else's wrong action cause you to do something you'll regret. Even worse, don't let someone else's wrong action turn you into jerk. That is giving them too much power over you.

I get that this is not easy. There are times where my emotions get the best of me. Most of those times involve parenting. During a full-blown meltdown by my son, he yelled at his mom. We sent him up to his room to calm down, and while in his room he yelled out something ugly. I lost it. I was so frustrated with his behavior! I found myself *yelling* at him about how we don't yell at our family. Like an Alannis Morrissette song, this moment felt ironic. I stopped mid yell and started laughing. My son was a little weirded out. I think he thought I had finally snapped. He looked at me puzzled, and when my laugh continued, he started laughing with me. He didn't have a fat clue why I was laughing, but laughter can be contagious. After I stopped laughing, I apologized and said we could talk later when he calmed down. It wasn't long before he called for me and was ready to apologize.

I don't always get this right, but it's my goal to not let others control my actions. On that day I apologized to my son for yelling at him, it didn't change the fact that his actions were wrong. He had to apologize as well. It's just that I don't want my response to someone else's reaction to change who I am.

Now here is why this is so important. The best of relationships can be transformed negatively in a moment. The best friendships can turn ugly quickly. The best family relationships can turn messy quickly. The best marriages can turn negative really quickly. One careless act can destroy years of great memories. When we feel offended, the inner jerk comes out swinging. Is there anyone in your life that you are no longer as close to as you once where and it's because of some type of drama? I do. Relationships are tricky. Humans are way more fragile than we let on. But what do you do if there is an issue and you just simply don't agree on it? In order to have relational health, you must put yourself in their shoes. If you don't, the jerk will thrive. Now to be clear, I'm writing about having empathy for those we disagree with. This is not advocating for remaining in an abusive relationship because you are trying to show them empathy. I hate that I have to include that disclaimer. Empathy does not mean we do not have boundaries. Empathy does not mean that we allow others to abuse us. I'm writing about having empathy for the people in your life that you just don't understand. I'm writing about having empathy for those you disagree with. If physical, emotional, or verbal abuse is involved, you can have empathy from a distance. That is, you should remove yourself from a harmful situation. I'm writing about empathy for those we love the most but because of differences we find a divide in our relationship.

There is a Scripture that speaks into this. It's written by Paul, who is a prime-time player in the Christian faith. Now here is something to think about when it comes to Paul and relationships. Paul started off persecuting Christians. He saw the light and became a Christian. Now all of the sudden he found himself having conversations with people he persecuted. Can you even imagine the awkward conversations he must have had? Paul had to wrestle through some relational tensions. This is what Paul wrote to some of the earliest Christians:

> Don't just pretend to love others. Really love them. Hate what is wrong. Hold tightly to what is good. (Rom. 12:9)

Did you catch what Paul said? Do not just pretend to love one another. Truly love each other. There are a lot of fakers out there. Don't be a person who says one thing to someone's face and then turns around and shares how you really feel behind their back. That's a jerk move. Really love people. At the same time hate what is wrong and hold tight to what is good. Okay, this screams empathy. In order to have healthy relationships, I must hold tightly to what is good. That is, I must choose to believe the best, honor others, and be grateful for what I have instead of focusing on what I don't.

There have been so many dividing issues that have found their way on social media. Whether it's gun-control laws, refugees, the Supreme Court's ruling on same-sex marriage, or the red Starbucks cups, people have opinions and they are often different than yours. Paul says, "Love people. Don't just pretend to love them. Really love them." At the same time you are to hold to what is good and hate what is evil. How do you do this?

Empathy.

There are some sins that are pretty clearly sins in the Bible. There are things that we should hold on to that are right, and there are things we should avoid that are wrong. When someone is involved in something that is wrong, we are called to still love them. That doesn't mean we agree with them. It doesn't mean we fully accept or fully reject them. It means we treat them how we would want to be treated. I hate sin. I hate the effects of sin. I hate how sin breaks us. I hate how sin lies to us and tells us to go into hiding. When we sin, we overestimates our ability to handle it while at the same time underestimates the consequences. Sin is always more costly than what we estimate. I hate sin.

We are to love what is right, and when someone loves something that is wrong, it should break our hearts. Whenever someone does something that is not God's best, our hearts should break for them. They are missing out on God's best. I may not have dealt with every sin and struggle that you have, but I can learn to show you empathy. I can relate to struggle. It may not be your struggle, but I know how difficult it is to overcome something that I deal with. Paul goes on to write:

> Love each other with genuine affection, and take delight in honoring each other. Never be lazy, but work hard and serve the Lord enthusiastically. Rejoice in our confident hope. Be patient in trouble, and keep on praying. When God's people are in need, be ready to help them. Always be eager to practice hospitality. (Rom. 12:10–13)

Paul gives us some great challenges for relationships. Love each other with genuine affection. Don't fake it. Really love one another. Take delight in honoring each other. Never be lazy. Now I don't know exactly what Paul is referencing here, but I'll tell you, it is lazy in relationships to dismiss people when you don't agree with them. That's easy. What's difficult is to engage and love someone who lives contrary to what you believe is right. It's easy to boycott, walk out on, block on social media, and dismiss everyone that doesn't think like us. It is incredibly challenging to live in community with people who you disagree with. Jerks focus on differences. Christians are to love those who are different. Again, that doesn't mean that we approve of their behavior. Loving someone and approving of everything they do are not the same thing. We can disagree and still be friends. Let's keep reading to see what Paul writes next.

> Bless those who persecute you. Don't curse them; pray that God will bless them. Be happy with those who are happy, and weep with those who weep. Live in harmony with each other. Don't be too proud to enjoy the company of ordinary people. And don't think you know it all! (Rom. 12:14–16)

Empathy is all over these verses. Instead of cursing, bless those who curse you. How? This is where God's love comes in. We can bless those who curse us when we realize that is what Jesus did for us. When we were at our worst, God loved us. From there we are to be happy with those who are happy and weep with those who weep. That's empathy. Paul calls it harmony. When we match our response to someone else's feelings, we show we care about them. When we bring empathy to someone's struggle, we experience harmony. Whenever there is disunity, there is a lack of harmony. Where there is a lack of harmony, there is a lack of empathy. Or it's a middle school choir. I kid, I kid. In order to grow in our empathy, we must follow the last part of that verse. Paul says, "Don't think you know it all." A lack of empathy is really pride in assuming that what we think is always right. If everyone you agree with is right and everyone you disagree with is an idiot, then you are assuming you are always right. That's pride. More on this in chapter 10.

Some personalities may come with more built-in empathy, but everyone can grow in empathy. In order to do so we must practice empathy. Empathy has four qualities. These are qualities that when practiced can drastically impact our relationships.

Four Qualities of Empathy

The Four Qualities of Empathy:

1. See the situation from their perspective.
2. Suspend your judgment of their view.
3. Recognize their emotion without dismissing it.
4. Communicate that emotion in a healthy way.

The first quality, seeing the situation from the other person's perspective, doesn't mean you agree with it. It means you are trying to understand. Don't curse them; bless them. They may not deserve it, but you don't deserve God's love and yet He gives it freely. Even when we are at our worst God loves us. If everyone you agree with is right and everyone you disagree with is an idiot, then you are assuming you are always right. Paul says don't do that.

The second quality is to suspend your judgment. Paul says, "Don't think you know it all." Believe the best about the other person. This is a choice. When someone hurts us, we need to ask questions, not form judgments. Asking questions helps us get to the truth. A judgment could be based on faulty information. People should be innocent until proven guilty. Take a pause and ask questions. Hope that you will find the truth. It might mean that the other person is in the wrong, or it could mean that you learn the hurt wasn't done on purpose.

The third quality of empathy is to recognize their emotion without dismissing it. Paul says be happy with those who are happy and weep with those who weep. I may not agree with your stance, but I can tell this upsets you, so I'm going to weep with you. That's empathy. It is a major jerk move to dismiss someone's emotion simply because it's different than yours. Telling someone they shouldn't cry, be upset, or get emotional about something is not healthy. Think about how you want to be treated. When you have emotions, how do you want others to treat you? I can't speak for you, but I want someone to understand where I'm coming from. I want someone to say, "I can see why that would stink." I don't want others to dismiss my emotions. Empathy is a bridge to relationships.

The final part of empathy is to communicate that emotion. Paul says to pray for those who persecute you. It is not healthy to keep your hurt inside. Sometimes you have to say it out loud, and the only person who is not going to give you any judgment in return is God. In counseling circles I've often heard how people solve their own problems when they simply talk about them out loud. Not always, but often a person gains understanding to their own situation when they talk about it with a safe person. In order to show empathy, I need to communicate that emotion. Saying things like, "I can see this upset you. I can imagine this is hard," allows the other person to see you care about them even if you disagree.

The amazing thing about empathy is that it can be learned. Like a muscle we can strengthen our empathy. By practicing empathy and the four qualities, we can learn to be more empathetic. It may not be easy for you, but it's so worth it. When it's not easy for you, think about how you would want someone to treat you on your worst day. We crave empathy, but we often serve vengeance. Jerks! Empathy is the antidote to the inner jerk. It causes you to take your eyes off yourself and to remember that the other person is a human in need of love.

Let's Wrap This Up

Paul then writes:

> Never pay back evil with more evil. Do things in such a way that everyone can see you are honorable. Do all that you can to live in peace with everyone. (Rom. 12:17–18)

Evil for evil does not get us anywhere. Wishing someone pain after they've done wrong is the opposite of what you want to happen when you've done something wrong. Treat others how you want to be treated is not some fortune-cookie idea or bumper-sticker slogan. It's a way of life. And nothing will show what you believe more than the way you want to treat other people after you've been hurt, angered, or offended. This doesn't mean that justice doesn't need to happen. If someone wrongs you, there may have to be a consequence. In thinking through that consequence, think through how you would want to be treated if you were guilty. Showing empathy doesn't mean the other person is off the hook. It means you are going to try and understand where they came from so you can walk with them. Justice may still need to happen. There can still be consequences, and you can have empathy.

The way you combat evil is by doing the opposite. When there is hatred, you bring love. Where there is discord, you bring peace. Where there is darkness, you bring light. Where there is selfishness, you bring generosity. Christians can do this because we have received this from Jesus. He brings love to our hatred, peace to our discord, light to our darkness, and generosity to our selfishness. If you have never received this from Jesus, then it's difficult to give it to others. If you have received and don't want to give it to others, you need to crucify the jerk. When we are hurt, all we can see is our hurt. Through Jesus, the great physician, I can give my hurt in return for healing. Until this happens, my hurt will blind me from seeing how my own actions are hurting others. We need to bring our hurt to Jesus, receive his love, and then we can love others through their hurt.

This takes practice. The more comfortable we are with someone, the less patience we have. It's easy to believe the worst, snap in frustration, or take for granted those that we love. Remember the honeymoon phase? We take for granted those we feel are going to be around us forever. That's a jerk move.

Paul then says, "Do all that you can to live at peace with everyone." Do everything in your power to live at peace with everyone. Now why is this so important? When you are upset at someone else, what are you focused on? Yourself. When someone has upset you, the tendency is to focus on how wrong they are for hurting you. It's easy when you are upset to focus on all the wrong they have done to you. We spend a lot of time thinking about how others have hurt us, but the truth is we do this because we are wired to think about ourselves a lot.

> Self-absorption in all its forms kills empathy, let alone compassion. When we focus on ourselves, our world contracts as our problems and preoccupations loom large. But when we focus on others, our world expands. Our own problems drift to the periphery of the mind and so seem smaller, and we increase our capacity for connection—or compassionate action. (Daniel Goleman, *Social Intelligence: The New Science of Human Relationships*)

I know the person who upset you is a jerk. I know they are annoying. I know they are a know-it-all. At some point in your life, you've been those things. When you were at your worst, how do you wish someone treated you? Treat others that way. Even if discipline needs to happen, think about how you would want to be disciplined if roles were reversed? If you were the guilty person, who would you want someone to discipline you? I know for me it would not include yelling and screaming. When I discipline my kids, I work hard at not disciplining them out of anger. All anger teaches is for those we love the most to fear us. Disciplining can include a time-out or break, losing something for a temporary time with the goal of being able to earn it back, or an action plan to work on an improved behavior.

Listen, when someone hurts you, the natural reaction is to react like a child and try to hurt them back. It may make you feel better in the moment, but it will not make you better at relationships. Empathy doesn't replace discipline. It doesn't mean that there aren't healthy consequences. For one couple where the husband broke his wife's trust, I asked them what would help build her trust back. From there we were able to come up with a plan. If he kept the plan, the goal was her trust would be regained. Up until they came up with a plan on how to regain trust, they were spending hours yelling at each other about the broken trust. It was unfruitful. They came to me with the conclusion that they had to break up. They left with hope that they could work things out.

When you are hurt by someone else, think about the golden rule. How would you want someone to treat you if you made this mistake? You cannot control them. You do you. That is, you work on yourself. You put yourself in their shoes. You find a way to have empathy toward them. You pray for them. Don't allow someone's bad behavior to change your good reactions. Kill the jerk!

The Win for this chapter: Copy the four qualities of empathy and put them some place where you will see them often. Whenever you see them, practice them until they become natural to you.

Questions for Further Reflection

1. Out of the four qualities of empathy, which one do you do the best?
2. Which one do you struggle with?
3. When have you seen someone show you empathy?
4. How can you practice showing empathy to others?

CHAPTER 4

Unmet Expectations Are Fuel for Jerks

Relationships are difficult! Whether it's marriage, friendship, coworkers, or family, it's difficult to live with others. One of the main reasons being in community with other people is difficult comes down to the fact that everyone is playing by a different set of life rules. Often these rules are not communicated. If you struggle getting along with someone, are constantly frustrated with someone, or feel disappointed by someone on a regular basis, then there is great potential it comes back to the rules in which you live life by.

You've spent your whole life learning to play by a certain set of rules. You've developed these rules from various sources: somewhere from your childhood, the entertainment you consumed, your understanding of God, and your friendships. Some of the rules were developed by your parents. Some were developed by your teachers. Some are developed by your personality. These are the most difficult rules because our personality makes us believe that everyone should view the world like we do.

We all have rules that we live by. These rules are so ingrained in us that we often don't know we are playing life by them. They aren't written down. They most likely have never been expressed. The rules that you have grown to live by are so ingrained in you that you do not realize what they are until you see someone break one of your rules. When someone breaks one of your rules, it's incredibly difficult to show them empathy. We think, *They should just know!* They don't know. They don't know because they cannot read your mind and because they are playing by a different set of rules.

Relationships are tough because both people are often playing by a separate set of rules. We are often punishing each other for breaking unwritten rules. Relationships will always be challenging because we are broken human beings, but they become so much more life giving and way less frustrating when we know the rules we are playing by.

As humans it is natural to assume people should just know "what I'm feeling." We think that because the rules to life are so clear to us. We think, *Only an idiot would not know that is breaking a rule.* So many of our relational issues come from unspoken rules we assume others should play by.

It is not fair to penalize someone for breaking a rule they didn't know existed. My pastor friend Freddy says it this way: "Don't give me a test I didn't know I was taking." What I often hear in relationships is, one person passive-aggressively leaves clues that they are hurting or their needs aren't being met. When the other person involved in the relationship doesn't pick up on their cues, they become offended. After months or years of frustration, this person finally snaps. When they do, it feels like it came out of nowhere to the other person involved. At that point it is almost always too late.

One couple I met with were speaking a completely different language even though they both spoke English. The issue at hand happened over the weekend. The wife desperately wanted some family time with her husband. She was tired from being alone with the kids all week. She asked if her husband would like to go on a family bike ride. He did not. He shared that he was tired from a long week. She took the kids on a bike ride and was furious at him. When we met, I encouraged both of them to meet in the middle when it comes to communication. He needed to listen better. At the same time she didn't communicate her expectations. She asked if he wanted to go on a bike ride. He didn't. If she had said, "I want to spend time with you and so would our kids, let's go on a bike ride," he would have potentially responded differently. In fact, once I translated for him what was being said, he was frustrated at himself. He missed the clues and wished he would have gone for that bike ride. At the same time, she realized that what she asked and what she really wanted were two different things.

The Power of Expectations

Nothing, and I mean nothing, will draw out the inner jerk more than unmet expectations. We all have expectations. Many of those expectations are unrealistic or are not communicated. For example, my all-time favorite movie is *Raiders of the Lost Ark*. As a kid I loved the trilogy of Indiana Jones. Loved it! I watched it more than any other movie series. When the crew who made the first three movies got back together to make a fourth film, I was out of my mind excited! Because I loved the first three movies, I had no doubt I would love the fourth. I went into the movie with high expectations. I couldn't wait to relive a part of my childhood. Instead, I watched two plus hours of George Lucas (writer and producer) destroying my childhood! When the movie ended, I was so upset I couldn't talk. In my family, movies are a communal event so we had a whole row of people with us. When I heard someone say it was a good movie, I immediately envisioned the scene from *Temple of Doom* where the bad guy pulls a beating heart out of a poor soul's chest. To make matters worse, she said, "That was a really funny movie. What wasn't there to like?" Um, Indiana Jones is not a comedy. Sure it has some humor in it, but it's *not a comedy*! I was fiery mad. I literally could not talk about the movie without getting angry. I had to change the subject when it was brought up for the rest of that day. I hated that movie more than any other movie experience in my life. I hated it so much I went back to see it a second time. Wait! What? Why? I was hoping that the second time viewing the movie would be better. It wasn't. I left the theater the second time just as angry. Why? Because expectations are powerful. Maybe you've given or received unhealthy expectations.

Expectations like

- You should know I needed you to do that. I shouldn't have to ask.
- If she really cared, she would have called me.
- You expect me to do everything!
- I was hurting and no one from the church reached out to me.
- You didn't invite me because you didn't want me there.

Whenever we do not have all the information, our brains complete the narrative. It's rarely helpful or accurate. It leads to unmet expectations. Unmet expectations destroy our ability to see things as they really are. I've had the same thing happen with movies I didn't care about. I left the theater entertained while others who had an invested interest in it left angry. It's not just movies. Unmet expectations destroy relationships. Whether it's because we expect marriage to be like a Nicholas Sparks novel or we think friendship should be like a TV show. You know, the one with the *Friends*. Unmet expectations can come from a myriad of different places. No matter where they come from, each person has to learn to manage their expectations.

In relationships unmet expectations destroy intimacy, lead to division, and are often the cause of conflict. You learn a lot about people when they don't have their expectations met. You learn just how big of a jerk a person has living inside of them. When someone doesn't get what they want, you will see their jerk come out swinging. You have rules. I have rules. Unspoken rules are resentments waiting to happen. Unspoken expectations are resentments waiting to happen. Unrealistic expectations are the cause of so many broken relationships.

Big Idea: Unspoken and unrealistic expectations are resentments waiting to happen.

Many have learned this the hard way. After a lifetime of disappointments, it's easy to conclude that expectations are evil. Some people have been so wounded by expectations that they simply hate everything. Their thought is if they always have low expectations, it will make the pain of unmet expectations that much easier. That may be true, but that is no fun to be around. Nobody enjoys being around someone who is negative. The answer is not to simply dismiss all expectations. We need expectations or we will not get anywhere in our relationships. We just need healthy, realistic expectations.

It's not wrong to have expectations. It is wrong to have unspoken and unrealistic expectations.

I expect drivers to follow the rules of the road. I get upset when they don't. I expect my kids to follow the rules we've set. When they don't, there is a consequence. I expect certain things out of myself. I have the expectation that when I wake up in the morning my breath is going to kick like Chuck Norris. Because I expect that, I brush my teeth before I talk to anyone in the morning. Killing all expectations leads to passive living. It's so easy to become numb to disappointments and thus simply go through the motions of life. There has to be a better way. I believe there is. Let's look more at why expectations are unmet.

Expectations are often unmet because they are

1. Unspoken
2. Unrealistic

The jerk inside thrives off other people breaking your unspoken and unrealistic expectations. In order to deal with the jerk, we must unearth our expectations. We will start with unspoken expectations and then move on to unrealistic expectations.

Unspoken Expectations

We all get upset. We all get upset and often the reason is because of broken expectations. It is impossible to communicate every expectation to every relationship. There are just too many. Instead, what we must practice is controlling ourselves when someone breaks an unspoken expectation.

It is unfair to punish someone for an unspoken expectation! It is unfair to punish someone for an unspoken expectation. That's not a typo. I wrote it twice so maybe it would sink in.

To punish someone because we haven't given clear expectations is like playing a game by different rules. Have you ever played a game like Uno or Monopoly where you played by a different set of rules than other people? We call these house rules. It is up to me to explain the house rules. When anyone breaks one of the house rules, it is then up to me to control myself in my response. This is not easy. The rules are so ingrained in us we will naturally respond in anger or frustration. When one of our rules for life is broken, it catches us so off guard that we freak out.

Everyone has an inner jerk, but every time someone doesn't meet your expectation, it's not the jerk's fault. Let me explain. When our expectations are not met, we often believe the worst. We jump to the worst possible conclusion and assume that the only reason someone would break that rule is because they are an idiotic jerk. The truth is a lot of the time we penalize well-meaning people for breaking our unspoken rules. Now who is the jerk?

It is unfair to get angry at someone for breaking an unspoken rule. The truth is a lot of the people in our lives are well-meaning people. They aren't intentionally trying to make our lives difficult. They simply are clueless to the rules we live by.

Whenever you feel angry, it comes back to someone breaking one of your rules. You can tell because the self-dialogue we often have about other people says something like, "I can't believe they did that! I would never do that to them." You would never do that to them because it's one of your rules. When you yell at, belittle, make fun of, tear down, or fuss at someone for breaking an unspoken rule, it's unfair. So the next time you feel frustrated ask yourself, "Have I ever communicated this?"

Think about the last thing someone did that frustrated you? Be honest. It's okay if it was something silly. It's okay if it was petty. It's okay if it was a big deal. Think about something someone did to frustrate you. Was it the way they loaded the dishwasher, forgot to unload the dishwasher, folded laundry, showed up late to a meeting, forgot to do something they said they would. What is it? Got something?

Now ask yourself, "Did I communicate my expectation before it was broken?" If not, then you have some work to do. There is a great chance that your jerk came out and unleashed on someone for breaking a rule you never communicated.

Killing the jerk means you have learned to control yourself when someone breaks one of your unspoken expectations. After all, you cannot control other people. You can only work on controlling yourself. Once you discover someone has broken one of your unspoken rules, it is up to you to communicate the expectation. Try to show some empathy to the other person. In your mind they are wrong, but from their perspective, they don't think they did anything wrong. All of the sudden they are being fussed at for not making you happy. Often, the other person is confused and will do anything to appease you. Other times the person will push back, and a fight will ensue. The issue is, when we lead out of anger, the other person rarely understands why we are upset. Until they understand why, they will only focus on who. The who is you. In the other person's mind, they will think you are impossible to please, temperamental, or difficult. They will focus on how you treated them and still miss out on what you were trying to communicate. If you want to help someone learn, you have to try a different approach. Instead of punishing someone for breaking one of your unspoken rules, work on communicating the issue. Work on being clear without attacking the other person. Work on sharing what's going on inside of you.

Now if you have communicated an expectation and it's still being unmet, the next key is to ask yourself if you have an unrealistic expectation. More on this in a moment. Before I get to that I want to point out that when it comes to managing expectations, it starts with you and not the other person. We so often get this wrong. We fail to work on the jerk because we feel justified when he comes out. Even when someone breaks one of your rules, it doesn't change the fact that you are responsible for yourself. Two wrongs truly don't make a right. You can be right and still be wrong. You can be right in your frustration but still wrong in how you respond. Now let's look at unrealistic expectations.

Unrealistic Expectations

Unrealistic expectations come when we expect someone to be something God did not intend for them to be. Don't try to take out of people what God put in them, and never try to put in them what God left out. It's unfair. Not everyone thinks like you. Not everyone puts away dishes like you. Not everyone folds laundry like you. Not every person has your gifts and talents. So often we get upset with others because we expect them to do what we do. That's not right!

For example, I am not good at building things. It does not come naturally for me. I have to read the instructions to make Kool-Aid. There are only three. I still read them every time. Often when I work with someone who is great at working on cars or fixing things around the house, they have a hard time understanding why I am so bad at it. I have worked on it, and I hope that I am becoming somewhat better, but I am truly horrible at it. Not too long ago I tried to replace a brake light on my car. I didn't want to bother anyone with this simple task and thanks to YouTube I had a tutorial on how to do it. I watched the video and then tried to change the brake light. Once I started, I immediately forgot what the second step was so I watched the video again, but this time I paused it right after the second step. This was going to be easy, and I was starting to feel some pride for doing something mechanical on my own. The bar is low. I'm truly horrible at it. Well, pride meet fall. I ended up replacing the wrong bulb. The one I replaced wasn't out. When I went to take the wrong bulb out, I shattered it. My hand started bleeding all over the trunk of my car. I spent way too long on this project, and it still wasn't done. In my attempt to fix something simple, I made it a complex mess. My brother came by, and I asked if he could help me. He replaced it in two minutes, and he didn't watch a single YouTube video. I'm good at other things.

Often our unmet expectations come from expecting people to do things like we do. In the same way you are not great at everything, others are not great at what comes more natural to you. My wife's personality type[1] doesn't have a lot of empathy. She is a logic-thinking, no-emotions, get-er-done type of person. I love her for it. On the other hand, I have a lot of empathy.[2] It's what makes me good at counseling. I have still had to do a lot of research, reading, and practice; but my empathy helps me help other people. It is unfair for me to expect my wife to have the same amount of empathy I do. She often doesn't know what to do with my emotions. Because of this I've had to learn to communicate

1 Enneagram 3

2 Enneagram 9

my expectations. Defining the conversation before the conversation is crucial in helping manage expectations. Before I start venting, I have to share, "I really need you to just listen and let me know this difficult" or "I'm looking for advice." When I communicate my expectations clearly, she happily tries her best to help. When I am looking for advice, I let her know that upfront. When I'm simply looking to vent, I let her know upfront. It is unfair for me to expect her to know what I need without saying it. My wife is a very caring person, but it's unfair for me to expect her to have the same degree of empathy I do. At the same time, it's unfair for her to expect me to fix things when they break around the house. In moments like this we label the other person a jerk when in all actuality we are expecting them to be something God didn't create them to be.

Whether it's the way you do chores, your personality quirks, or how you communicate, you have to embrace that it's okay for others to do it differently than you do. There is more than one way to do almost everything. You can have control or you can have a healthy relationship, but you cannot have both. When you continually punish a person for doing things differently than you do, you become the problem.

So many of our relational issues come from unrealistic expectations. God did not make us all the same. In fact, He intentionally left certain gifts out of each person so that we would need each other. Look at what Scripture says:

> But in fact God has placed the parts in the body, every one of them, just as he wanted them to be. If they were all one part, where would the body be? As it is, there are many parts, but one body. (1 Cor. 12:18–20)

In this verse our giftedness is compared to parts of the body. Some people are hands and the get-er-done type people. Some people are mouths and are gifted to communicate. Some people are brains and are more gifted to think logically through things. Some people are hearts and are more in tune with their emotions. Some people are butts. Don't put the butts down. The butt is incredibly important. It's not glamorous, but when it's broken, your whole world doesn't work properly. Sleeping, sitting, walking, and going to the bathroom become incredibly painful when the butt is broken. The butt is behind the scenes, but it is no less important. The gifts you have are because God intentionally placed them in you to help others. The people in your life who are built differently than you are there to help you not make your life more frustrating. It is unfair to expect something from someone that God left out.

To be clear this is talking about giftedness and not sin. Do not use this chapter as an excuse to not practice killing your inner jerk. For example, do not say, "God did not make me patient, therefore you are just going to have to deal with my outbursts." That is not what this verse is talking about. This verse is talking about the gifts that God has given or not given you. Selfishness is not a gift. So much of our frustrations with other people come from the fact that we have unrealistic expectations. We expect people to act, react, think, and do things like we do.

Imagine just for a moment what it would be like to live with someone constantly getting angry at you for an unrealistic expectation. You might even think about someone who has done that to you. How did it make you feel? How does it feel to do something to the best of your ability only to have someone else tear you down or belittle you? How does it feel to have someone get angry at you when you didn't mean to upset them? In fact, you would do anything for this person and yet they get upset with you for simply being you. Are you there? Do you know this feeling?

Now think about what it's like to live with your unrealistic expectations. When an expectation is not met, the inner jerk feels justified to come out. You might rationalize it or justify it, but your unrealistic expectations are toxic to healthy relationships.

Here's a question to think about: would you enjoy life if others treated you the way you treat them? Sure, they may be in the wrong, an idiot, or clueless, but that doesn't mean you are no longer responsible for how you treat them. What's it like living with you?

Here's the deal: is the person you are frustrated with trying to frustrate you? If not, then you need to examine your expectations. For example, did the person intentionally try to harm you or upset you? If they did, then you have a problem. It is very realistic to expect people to treat you with respect, honor, and care. If someone is an abusive relationship, they should leave and seek help. It's realistic to expect people to respect you. That's not what this is about. Unrealistic expectations deal with the everyday annoyances that draw out our inner jerk.

According to NPR's Joe Palca, author of *Annoying: The Science of What Bugs Us*, "Everyone is annoyed by something. Many of us are annoyed by lots of things. Most of these annoyances have more to do with our personal sensitivities—our neuroses, our upbringings, our points of view—than any objective 'annoying' quality.'"

Translation: what annoys you is more about you than the other person. Unrealistic expectations are a breeding ground for annoyances. We often get annoyed because someone does something different than us. In marriages I see a lot of spouses go level 10 angry when their spouse does a chore different than they do. You can have control in your relationship or you can have growth, but you cannot have both. Instead of fussing at a spouse who does a chore different, try celebrating the fact they helped. I know some reading this won't like that. I don't know another option. You cannot control other people. You can however work on controlling yourself. Think about it, do you work better when you have a cheerleader or a critic speaking to you? You should be the biggest cheerleaders for the people you love. When you have healthy expectations, you become a safe person to be around. When you don't, the people in your life will set up barriers in order to not be hurt by you. If you want your friends and family to come to you with things, then you have to be safe person for them to come to. It's unrealistic to think that you can fuss at, yell at, or freak out at someone on a regular basis and yet expect them to still come to you with the sensitive details of their life.

Feeling constantly criticized for being yourself is exhausting. The jerk makes it difficult to see someone else's perspective. Our expectations are so strong that when someone breaks them we instantly jump to the fact they are the problem. Before you react to someone not meeting your expectations, think about what it would feel like to be on the other side of you. How would you feel if someone responded the way you want to? Would it bring you closer or further away from the other person?

Agreeing on Expectations

Once you learn to communicate realistic expectations, the next step is to agree on the expectations. It is not fair to put an expectation on someone if they do not agree to it. The key is to express expectations and then agree on a what's realistic. We shouldn't demand someone else to meet our expectations. We can't force our expectations on others. In healthy relationships, both people will willingly find a compromise and agree on the expectations.

At the church I work at, I am the primary teaching pastor. One of the single best decisions I ever made was to hire an executive pastor. Scott is gifted where I am not. He also has a completely opposite personality than me. I'm the gas, and he's the brake. When it comes to ideas, I build the boat while it's in the water and he makes sure everything is perfect before the boat ever leaves the shore. We work really well together, but it takes a lot of compromise. We have agreed on the expectations. I don't expect him to preach, and he doesn't expect me to run the business side of the church. We both have freedom to speak into the other person's expertise, but neither of us oversteps our grounds. Having him on my staff has made this by far my favorite season of ministry.

I write all of that to simply say, no matter the relationship you can have healthy expectations. It's not about one person winning. It's not about one person getting everything they want. It's about compromising and agreeing to healthy expectations.

Before You Leave This Chapter

The next time you feel your blood boiling because someone did not meet your expectations, ask the following:

1. Have I communicated this expectation before?
2. Am I being realistic with this expectation?
3. Have we agreed on these expectations?

Remember, you cannot control other people. So much of our anger stems from control. Unmet and unrealistic expectations stem from control. You cannot control others. You have to work on controlling yourself. The inner jerk will always focus on other people and how they make you feel. To see if you are being unrealistic with your expectations ask, "Am I trying to put in something that God left out?" That is, am I trying to put in my natural gifts into someone else? Am I trying to force someone to be someone God did not intend for them to be? The final thing is to analyze if you've agreed upon the expectations. Expectations are only valid when both parties agree upon them.

Having some standards that both people agree upon is crucial for managing expectations. In the next chapter we are going to dive into conflict. The inner jerk thrives in unruly conflict. When expectations are not met, conflict thrives. But before we go there, here are some questions for reflection. Remember the jerk always wants everyone else to change, but true life change starts with you.

The Win for this chapter: Make a date to talk about your uncommunicated expectations. Either with a friend, relative, spouse, or another close relationship, find the time to talk through expectations.

Questions for Further Reflection

1. When have you felt the sting of uncommunicated expectations? How did that make you feel?
2. When have you felt the sting of unrealistic expectations? How did that make you feel?
3. Identify one area where you have not communicated your expectations clearly?
4. Identify one unrealistic expectation you have?
5. How does it make you feel reflecting on your uncommunicated or unrealistic expectations?
6. What are you willing to do to clearly communicate your expectations?
7. What are you willing to do to change your unrealistic expectations?

CHAPTER 5

Rules of Engagement

Every relationship has conflict. We know this and yet we often deny or ignore the conflict in our life. Sixty-nine percent of conflicts are never solved. Ninety percent of conflicts are about figuring out where to eat. One of those stats is true, and one is meant to be funny. Conflict is an inevitable part of every relationship. When expectations are not met, the result is conflict. Even when we practice communicating our expectations and making sure our expectations are realistic, we will still have conflict. We are human. Conflict is not the problem. It's the way we deal with conflict that is the issue.

So often our conflicts do not get solved because of how we react to conflict. To kill the jerk, you must believe that the person on the other side of the conflict is a decent human being who is not intentionally trying to make your life horrible. They might be bringing hurt to the party, but it's because they are hurting. They might be bringing selfishness to your relationship, but it's because they are hurting. They may not be doing something the way you would, but are they intentionally trying to destroy your life by the way they load the dishes? We cannot control them, and we should not allow other's bad behavior to control us. We need to learn to treat others how we wish to be treated. This goes for how we bring up conflict and respond to conflict.

The question is, how do we have healthy conflict? To have healthy conflict you have to intentionally kill the jerk. That is, you must work on yourself. You cannot control what other people do. When we intentionally work on learning to control ourselves, we can have healthy conflict even when others are unhealthy.

I'm convinced that conflict should be more like the games we play than a street fight. Please note the games I'm talking about are board games, video games, or sports. I'm not referencing manipulative games jerks play to get back at others or to try and get their own way. That's unhealthy.

Games are meant to be fun. When you first open up a new board game, what is the first thing that you do? If you are like me, you read the rules first thing. This is crucial! If you do not understand the rules, the game is not fun. In the same way when someone plays a familiar game by a different set of rules, calamity ensues. I'm talking taking-off-the-earrings, pulling-out-the-brass-knuckles, ending-the-relationship type of drama ensues. Have you ever played a game like Monopoly or Uno with someone who plays by a different set of rules? It's infuriating! Whenever I play with someone who plays by a different set of rules, I immediately go back and look at the rule book. I don't care what your house rules are Timmy, if it's not the official rules, you are wrong. Who is Timmy? I don't know. It just felt like something a Timmy would do.

In order for a game to be fun there are rules that each person must abide by. When you play by the rules, the game can be fun. When someone breaks the rules or plays by a different set of rules, chaos ensues. When everyone understands the rules, plays together, and fights fair for the good of the relationship, you have healthy conflicts.

Before a boxing match a little referee stands between two giants and says, "Let's have a clean fight." He then goes on to give some rules for the fight. He says things like, "No rabid punches," "No blows below the belt," etc. The whole point of a fight is to punch someone so hard you knock them out, and yet they start the fight under the instructions to have a clean fight. That feels like an oxymoron. Not all of the time, but the vast majority of the time when two boxers both play by the rules, when the match is over, they embrace in the middle of the ring and congratulate each other.[3] What if our conflicts ended the same way? What if at the end of a conflict we could hug it out and remain friends? I believe we can when we play by the rules and have a clean fight.

When two people in relationships agree on the rules of engagement and then commit to keep the rules, you have a chance to have healthy conflict. Without some healthy rules a conflict becomes like a street fight. Everyone is fighting however they can to win, and in the end no one wins. Feelings are hurt, relationships are damaged, and even if someone wins, the relationship takes a beating. Conflict shouldn't be that way. We should be able to disagree and still be friends. Conflicts are simply games that we have to figure out the rules in order to win.

Think of these as rules to a game. Do not think of these as rules like laws. There is a difference. Rules to a game help us know how to play. Your relationships should be fun. With some healthy rules, relationships can be fun. Without

---

[3] For a great example of this watch the original *Karate Kid.* Even though there is debate to whether or not the crane kick is legal, the point is at the end of the match, Daniel wins the respect of his opponent. And, yes, I know *Karate Kid* is not a boxing movie.

healthy rules the inner jerk runs wild. When two inner jerks come out in a conflict, nobody wins.

Examples of Rules

What are some examples of potential rules? Real rules that work in a conflict. You do not have to adopt my rules. Feel free to come up with your own.

Rules of Engagement:

1. *Absolutely no absolutes*: I realize I used an absolute in this rule, but remember these are supposed to be fun. An absolute is a surefire way to add fuel to an argument. It goes like this:

   Person 1: You always leave me out.

   Person 2: No, I don't! I include you all the time. I included you last week!

   Person 1: *You're not listening to me*! You never listen to me!

   Person 2: I am listening to you! *You just don't make any sense*!

   You get the idea. The truth is, an absolute is rarely absolutely true. Instead of saying words like *always* or *never* work on talking about what is really upsetting you. Instead of saying, "You always," say, "I feel." I feel left out. I feel hurt. I feel upset. Communicating what is going on inside of you is way more healthy than declaring someone always or never does something.
2. *Do not bring up the past*: This is a rule for an argument. There may be times where you have to talk

about the past in order to find healing and move on. During an argument, bringing up the past is an unfair fighting tactic. I'm a middle child, and stereotypically, we like to argue. Not only that but we like to win an argument. It's an unfair fighting tactic to bring up the past. It's an attempt to change subjects and win.

3. *No name-calling*: Name-calling does not help solve a conflict. It escalates it. Quite frankly, resorting to name-calling is a sign of immaturity. When we don't get our way, the jerk insists on having a tantrum. Name-calling won't solve the issue. The people we love the most should be the people we speak to the best.
4. *Interruptions are a no-go*: Interruptions are a sign that we are not listening. Listen to what the other person is saying. Wait to respond. Interrupting doesn't win. Interrupting shows that the other person isn't as valuable. That's not a good thing.
5. *Raise a glass, not a voice*: Yelling is a form of intimidation. When a person is losing a conflict, some rise up like a bear to try to verbally intimidate or win. Yelling is an unfair fighting tactic.
6. *Shutting down is for computers, not people*: Some people are wired to shut down when a conflict arises. This feels natural to some, but it does not help solve the conflict.

What happens when rules are established and one person fights unfair by breaking a rule? The penalty for not following the rules is a relationship that is no fun. Remember this is like a board game. The reward of fighting fair and establishing rules is fun in the relationship. It's having a conflict and feeling closer to each other after it's done. It's the difference between playing a game like basketball with people who understand the rules and playing with that one joker who travels, double dribbles, and doesn't give a rip that he's not playing within the rules. His name is probably Timmy. I kid, I kid. I have no issue with any Timmys. I'm just trying to be funny. That takes us to the big idea for this chapter.

Big Idea: Conflicts can be healthy when rules of engagement are practiced.

It may seem like a pipe dream, but conflict doesn't have to be avoided or messy. It should be handled with care, and a few rules of engagement help do just that. Before you build your rules, there is one thing you need to consider. It has to do with your personality.

Stuffers vs. Spillers

Without rules for engagement many families, relationships, and friendships simply ignore conflict. Difficult things do not get discussed. Tense moments are buried deep with hope they will never surface. This is not a safe relationship or home. In order to feel safe, you must trust that the relationship is strong enough to fix issues in the relationships.

For others, without rules of engagement when a conflict arises, it's an all-out war. This is also not a safe environment. Often when people allow anger to control their emotions, it causes others to avoid or flat out hide information. When someone is a walking time bomb, those around them are all too careful not to make them explode.

The rules of engagement are especially helpful for our personality types. We should not bury issues because we are afraid of conflict, and we should not explode on people every time we are bothered.

Depending on your personality, you are either a stuffer or a spiller. When emotions get high, we tend to react in one of two ways: stuffers or spillers.

Stuffers: A stuffer is someone who stuffs feelings deep down, avoids conflict, and shuts down during conflict. When conflict arises, a stuffer may shut down and when pressed could use the phrase, "Nothing is wrong. I'm just tired."

Spillers: A spiller is someone who spews when emotions get high. They want to talk it out. Maybe prone to raising their voice. When a conflict arises, they get chatty. Spillers want to talk through conflict even if it means TALKING THROUGH A CONFLICT!

When a stuffer stuffs feelings, they only remained buried for so long. Eventually, the feelings come out, and when they do, look out. A stuffer may bring up an issue that has long passed. It could be weeks, months, or, in some cases, years old.

When a spiller experiences feelings, they want to get them out quickly. They don't like holding on to conflicts. They will talk and talk even if it means talking the issue to death. When a spiller is angry, everyone feels it. When a spiller is anxious, everyone feels it. Emotions spill onto anyone and everyone that is nearby.

With the right set of rules and a little bit of compromise both spillers and stuffers can learn to communicate during a conflict. The key is to recognize that you are taking a step toward having a healthy conflict. It may not be easy, but having a set of rules will help. When a stuffer feels safe, they are more likely to communicate. Often stuffers stuff because they are afraid of conflict. Conflict hasn't gone well in the past. Or they don't trust themselves in conflict. Without rules a stuffer has experienced their emotions out of control.

A spiller without any rules can over-communicate their feelings. Even if it means railroading the other person, talking over them, interrupting, or not respecting someone's opinion or space.

With a few rules that are mutually agreed upon, you can manage expectations and have healthy conflict. A tricky part about this is that not everyone will agree to rules, and you will know some people who it's simply impossible to form any rules for conflict.

It is 100 percent not fair to tell other people what rules they should live by. You can still live by your rules even when others don't have rules for their conflict. When they go low, remember to treat them how you would want to be treated, not how you are feeling. We cannot force our rules on others. We can simply establish some rules and play the game of life by them. Relationships become fun when both people agree upon the rules and keep them. When one or both people do not play by the rules, dysfunction ensues.

The next chapter is a look at how jerks fight. It builds upon this chapter. Before we get there let's reflect by answering some questions about this chapter.

The Win for this chapter: Who is the person that is closest to you? Sit down with them and define some rules of engagement. It's okay if you don't have a lot of conflict. If you are close enough, you will have conflict at some point. If you have a list of rules, you'll be prepared for when that day comes.

Questions for Further Reflection

1. What is your favorite game to play?
2. Are you more of a stuffer or a spiller?
3. How would having a few rules of engagement have helped you in past conflicts?
4. Out of the examples for rules of engagement, which one applies the most to you? Why?
5. Which one of the rules applies the least?
6. What is one rule you will apply to yourself ASAP?
7. What rule would you add to the list given?

CHAPTER 6

How Jerks Fight

Most people do not experience healthy conflict because they have never trained themselves to handle conflict. When it comes to conflict, most of us act like untamed animals. You weren't born with claws, so you shouldn't fight like an animal. We either fight like lions or run away like zebras screaming, "Panic and run!" You are more than an animal. And if you are a Christian, this is especially important because we are called to love others the way that Jesus has loved us. I love the quote by Charles Stanley: "Our emotions are never to rule over us. We're to be the master of our responses and reactions. The moment we feel the intense emotions of anger, the first thing we must ask ourselves is, 'How should I respond?' Ideally, our emotions will be filtered through a will that's bent toward God's purposes and commandments. However, if the filter has been damaged or has never been put in place, emotions will usually give rise to behavior that's unchecked. And emotions not subjected to godly thinking tend to run amok and cause great damage eventually." Preach!

This is why we need Scripture. It's a foundation to give us direction. Without it we are like the Wild West when it comes to our emotions. When we feel hurt, we naturally want to hurt others back. Thus, problems aren't solved, they are escalated.

Look at what Paul said about dealing with those you disagree with:

> Do not repay anyone evil for evil. Be careful to do what is right in the eyes of everyone. (Rom. 12:17)

Do not repay anyone evil for evil. The word *anyone* means any one. That includes your family, coworkers, neighbors, friends, and enemies. This is not easy to do! The natural thought is, if you are nice to me, I will be nice to you, but if you are mean to me, then I get to pay you back. For Christians it is essential that we don't treat others the way they treat us. We are called to treat others the way Jesus has treated us. We are called to treat others the way we wish to be treated. I'm not to love others the way they have loved me. I'm to love others the way God has loved me and how I wish they would treat me. I'm not to forgive others as they have forgiven me. I'm to forgive others as God has forgiven me. Over my lifetime God has had to forgive me a bunch. Over my lifetime God has loved me through some pretty stupid and selfish decisions. Thank God for His forgiveness and grace. Because I'm loved by God, I can love others.

Paul then says, "Be careful to do what is right in the eyes of everyone." Now this is not saying that we become people pleasers. Paul's point is that in every situation respond in a way that points other people to Jesus. When it comes to conflict, you can have healthy conflict that represents God well. That's where your rules of engagement come in. It doesn't mean the other person will respond well. It doesn't mean the other person will agree. You cannot control other people. You can only work on controlling yourself. At some point someone will disagree with you. How you handle that disagreement says a lot about you.

In order to do that, well, you have to understand the unhealthy ways you respond to conflict. Even with the rules of engagement, if you are not aware of how you respond to conflict, you'll struggle responding in a Christlike way. The rules of engagement are crucial, but when desperation rises standards fall. That is, when you feel really offended, it's easy to throw your own rules out the window.

When it comes to conflict, we often live by repaying people evil for evil. We justify our wrong behaviors because of the way we have been treated. The issue is that retaliation doesn't fix a conflict. In fact,

Retaliation escalates conflict.

The jerk tells us that we will feel better if we get a person back for hurting us. The jerk is a liar. We don't feel better, and problems go unsolved when we retaliate. Retaliation escalates a conflict because when both people are trying to get back at each other, nothing healthy happens. When we feel hurt, it's easy to throw our rules of engagement out and think, *They aren't playing nice, so I won't either*. That's problematic. You are better than that. I believe you are better than that. I know it's not easy, but one person's jerk of an attitude should not change who you are and who you ultimately want to be.

Three Ways Jerks Retaliate

Now, when it comes to conflict, humans retaliate one of three ways. We may change our tactics based on our relationship or fears; but for the most part, when you feel hurt, you respond in one of three ways.

Three Natural Reactions to Conflict

1. Passive

   The passive person (or martyr)—blames other people or situations for feeling miserable

   The passive person will retreat in conflict, avoid conflict, but quietly stew over how others have made them unhappy. Characteristics of passive behavior are the silent treatment, shutting down, retreating, and avoiding.

   The passive person feels like a martyr. Whenever conflict happens, they give an excuse. The passive person may say, "You are right, I'm lazy. I just can't help it. My parents were lazy, and that's why I am lazy. Or "You are right I am selfish, but I'm selfish because I was never treated right as a kid." Or even worse, "You are right I'm no good, and I'll never be any good. It's not my fault." The passive person wants to blame others for how they feel instead of taking ownership of their feelings. Do everything you can to fight against a victim or martyr mindset. It will hold you back. You are not helpless. It may be tough; but blaming others, wallowing in sorrow, and feeling sorry for oneself doesn't help.

To the passive person it's important to understand that today is not good or bad. Today is an opportunity to make a choice. We can choose to be martyrs of our circumstances, or we can choose to make the most out of every opportunity. Even when bad things happen to us we can choose to learn from them or we can choose to wallow in them. Either way you have a choice to how you respond to difficulty. If today doesn't feel great, then make it great! We do not control every circumstance, but we can control our attitude. Your attitude determines the quality of your destination.

When someone hurts you, it does not hurt them to become passive. It hurts you and makes the relationship unsafe. Please don't feel beat up by this. I'll share how to grow in this area later. For now let's keep looking at the three natural responses to conflict.

2. Passive-Aggressive

"Behind the smile, a hidden knife!" This is an ancient Chinese proverb describing passive-aggressive behavior.

A passive-aggressive person will avoid the person in conflict but find subtle ways to hurt them.

The passive-aggressive person attacks in a passive way. Common ways a passive-aggressive person deals with conflict is intentional procrastination. When a person is passive-aggressive, they will often turn in work late or wait until the last minute in an attempt to get back at the other person. A passive-aggressive person will look for ways to hurt the person they are in conflict with while at the same time still looking good. They won't hurt the other person in an obvious way. It will be subtle or hidden. For married couples this could be when the spouse intentionally withholds intimacy by saying, "I have a headache," in order to try and hurt the other person. In friendship it could be when the person intentionally doesn't return a text. At work it could come out in a myriad of ways. The passive-aggressive person at work will do what they can to sabotage a meeting or assignment in a subtle way. It won't come across as blatant disrespect, but it will hurt progress.

I once heard a story about a wife who was passive-aggressive with her husband. Whenever there was a conflict, she would shut down and stew quietly. To get back at her husband she would clean the toilets with his toothbrush while he was at work. He never knew.

Talking about people behind their back, withholding something from a person, not saying what is really going on, talking about people on social media without naming names, shutting down by giving the silent treatment, or hurting someone without them knowing are forms of passive-aggressiveness. When you won't talk about the problem but you create a new problem, you become the problem.

Passive-aggressive behavior is a jerk move because it doesn't help the relationships. It may make you feel better because you are hurting the other person, but in reality you are creating an unsafe world. A better option would be to deal with the problem. Hurt people hurt people, but healthy people point the way to healing. You get to choose what type of person you would like to be. Let's look at the third way we respond to conflict.

3. Aggressive

   The aggressive person will respond in conflict by attacking the other person.

   The goal of the aggressive person is to win at all costs. When they are hurting, they will pull out all stops to win. Some examples of an aggressive person in conflict include bringing up the past, changing subjects, attacking where it hurts the most, bullying or intimidation, raising your voice or yelling.

   The aggressive person may win an argument, but they continually lose the war. The only thing an aggressive person communicates is, "I'm the only person that matters in this conversation, and I will make you agree with me." That's unhealthy!

   At times we don't mean to be aggressive. There is a thin line behind being passionate and being aggressive. We can and should be passionate about things but not at the expense of the relationship. Aggressive reactions to conflict create unsafe environments. The people on the other side of the aggression do not know what will upset an aggressive person, so they will constantly feel unsafe.

Now that we have briefly covered each one, which one are you? Your response may be difficult to face, but it's the only way to move forward in a healthy way. Don't feel bad about how you respond. Take charge and do something about it. Own it! You might be a mixture of the three. You also may respond differently depending on the environment. Do not let that throw you. Try to pick the one that is your most natural go-to reaction. Now that you know how you respond, make a choice to respond in a healthy way. You cannot control other people, but you can attempt to control yourself.

When conflict happens, how you respond to conflict is just as important as the issue at hand. Jerks cannot see how they are responding because they are focused on what the other person has done. That is why responding instead of reacting is so important. That's the big idea for this chapter.

Big Idea: Learn to respond instead of react to conflict.

The natural reaction to conflict often accelerates the conflict. I've learned the hard way that reacting poorly to situations and people in my life doesn't change anything. A poor reaction doesn't change anyone's mind. It doesn't cause them to respect or agree with me. A poor reaction doesn't fix the problem, it makes it worse. Life is better when we don't react to every negative thing around us. Instead of reacting let's work on ourselves. When we do the hard work of discovering how to respond instead of react, we bring an inner peace to drama. We make things worse by poorly handling conflict. When we run away from conflict, we delay fixing the problem. When we refuse to communicate clearly, we confuse the problem. When we yell, we become the problem. When we react to conflict, we tend to react passively, passive-aggressively, or aggressively. That's unhealthy! A healthy response to conflict can put out a relational fire.

Look at what Paul says next:

> If it is possible, as far as it depends on you, live at peace with everyone. (Rom. 12:18)

As far as it depends on you, live at peace with everyone. You cannot control other people. You can't. You cannot control if someone is nice to you or mean. You cannot control if someone is passive, passive-aggressive, or aggressive. All you can do is work on controlling yourself. I love the quote by Jonathan Edwards: "Resolved: that all men should live for the glory of God. Resolved second: that whether others do or not, I will." Don't let someone drag you into their mess. Don't let someone else have so much control over you that it changes who you want to be.

As far as it depends on you, live at peace with everyone. Translation? Some people will be ugly in conflict, but don't let them drag you down with them. Don't react to their reaction. Find a healthy way to respond to their reaction. I'm going to choose to live in peace whether you want to or not. I'm going to choose to be healthy in relationships. I love the following idea:

> You have $86,400 in your account and someone stole $10 from you. Would you be upset and throw all of the $86,390 away in hopes of getting back at the person that took your $10? Or move on and live? Right, move on and live. See, we have 86,400 seconds in every day so don't let someone's negative 10 seconds ruin the rest of the 86,390. Don't sweat the small stuff, life is bigger than that. (Unknown)

As far as it depends on me, I'm going to do what I can to live at peace with everyone. The only reason I can do this is because Jesus first did it for me. He pursued me when I was at my worst. He gave me grace when I deserved wrath. Jesus also didn't chase after those who wanted to leave. He didn't chase after Judas or the thousands who left because his teaching was too difficult. In the parable of the prodigal son, we read that the God figure in the story ran toward the sinner coming home. I believe that's an accurate picture. Jesus loves us so much he will run to us to welcome us home. At the same time, he loves us so much he will let us leave. He keeps the door open for a return, but he doesn't force love. I want to be like Jesus. I want to be healthy enough to love those who are wrong, but at the same time healthy enough to let them leave. I don't always get this right, but I aim to be a person who can respond instead of react to conflict.

When you learn to respond to conflict, you choose to be healthy. A healthy response may be, "I need some time to process this. Let's talk later." An unhealthy response is, "Nothing is wrong. I'm just tired." Liar! A healthy response is, "That hurt my feelings, did I do something to hurt you?" A healthy response is to communicate what is going on inside of you without attacking the other person.

So when someone comes at you in an unhealthy way, you have to learn how to respond in a healthy way. Why? Because evil for evil doesn't solve the problem. Tit for tat doesn't solve problems. In the moment it may make you feel better, but if it further damages the relationship you've lost.

Let me ask you what you'd rather be. Would you rather be right but alone or in healthy relationships because of the way you handle conflict? It takes some work, but you can become great at relationships so that conflict doesn't derail you. It won't come easy, but nothing worth having ever does. It is the epitome of entitlement to dismiss someone because you disagree with them.

Not everyone wants healthy relationships. Some people will choose to be unhealthy because it helps them feel in control. That's on them. I don't want to let other people control my emotions. When someone chooses an unhealthy reaction, I don't have to let it control me. I don't have to show up to every party I'm invited to. If it's unhealthy or toxic, then I can decline the invitation.

Paul makes this clear next. Look at what he says:

> Do not take revenge, my dear friends, but leave room for God's wrath, for it is written: "It is mine to avenge; I will repay," says the Lord. On the contrary: "If your enemy is hungry, feed him; if he is thirsty, give him something to drink. In doing this, you will heap burning coals on his head." (Rom. 12:19–20)

This is so life changing! As long as it depends on you, bring peace to your relationships. When someone is unhealthy, you have to bring health. You and I get to learn to respond to conflict instead of reacting to it. If your enemy is hungry, bring him food. If your enemy is thirsty, bring him something to drink. Translation: As long as it's up to you, bring peace where there is conflict. As long as it's up to you, bring love where there is hate. As long as it's up to you, bring empathy where there is division. After all, we are called to treat others like we want to be treated, not how we are feeling.

This is where the pushback may come. The thought is, if we don't avenge ourselves, fight back, or react, then we are letting the other person off the hook. This is where trusting God is crucial. It's God's job to judge and our job to love. The question is, do you trust God to take care of you? We cannot handle judging. We often make the wrong judgments, and even when we are right, we become consumed with anger. We cannot make the right judgments because we have a limited perspective. God, on the other hand, has an unlimited perspective. We can trust when he judges it will be fair. Be sure that if someone really wronged you, then Jesus has your back. In order to not allow the offense to consume you, it's crucial to bring love when we receive hate. The truth is that hate for hate doesn't change anyone. Jesus offers a better way.

How to Respond in Conflict

The first step is to identify how you naturally react to conflict. Once you understand it, then you can work on becoming more healthy. That's crucial because you cannot control others. Knowing how you respond may also help you establish some healthy rules of engagement. Once you are self-aware enough to know how you make others feel, you can establish a rule to help you think differently. At the same time we need to learn what the proper way to respond to those who bring unhealthy reactions to conflict. Understanding how to respond to someone who brings an unhealthy reaction is important. I've included a brief description of how we can respond to unhealthy conflict and then some thoughts on what this looks like practically.

How to Respond in Conflict:

1. Passive people need to hear, "That is tough, now what are you going to do about it?"

2. Passive-aggressive people need to hear, "I feel you are upset. We can talk when you choose to be responsible and tell me what is really going on."
3. Aggressive people need to hear, "I will only talk to you when you choose to be respectful."

The Passive Person

The passive person needs to hear empathy. They need to hear they matter. At the same time you cannot allow their bad behavior to drag the relationship down. Don't get sucked into their victim mentality. Empathy goes a long way. Let them know you understand it's tough, but life is tough. Ask them to think through what are they going to do about it?

Now the passive person may not feel they can do anything about it. This is where you need to consider establishing a boundary. For now, think about how you can stay strong in your response. When someone is being passive, respond by giving them empathy and then encourage them to do something. For example, "I can only imagine that was difficult for you. What are you willing to do to make it better?" If they respond with, "I don't know" or "Nothing," then they have found their identity in being passive. It's important to encourage them by saying, "I believe you are better than this. I believe you know what to do, and I'll help you do that. Let me know when you are ready to do something about this." Then you move on.

That may sound harsh, but a passive person has to know that they cannot drag you down. They may feel powerless, but you cannot react to their lack of confidence. I know this isn't easy, but it's doable when we practice responding instead of reacting. Just know you cannot work more on their problems than they do. This is why it's so important to encourage them to take ownership of their reactions and do something about it.

In my pastoral counseling sessions, I've had to learn this the hard way. There were people who were so used to being miserable they didn't see a way out. I would give practical insight, and the next time we met they had not applied anything they learned. It got to the point where I was being drained of life. Finally, I established a rule for meeting with people. Each time we meet I will give a homework assignment. If a person is not willing to do the homework, then we won't meet. Now I don't leave them hanging. I will recommend a professional counselor or other support that they might need. I care about people, but I care enough that I want them to find healing. The homework I give is practical and for the most part manageable. The point is, I cannot work on someone else's problem more than they do. When someone is willing to do some work, it shows that they aren't being passive about their circumstances. That leads to the passive-aggressive person.

The Passive-Aggressive Person

The passive-aggressive person needs to be pursued and listened to. The problem is they have a hard time saying what is really wrong. They are so afraid of conflict they would rather attack than deal with the issue.

When I help someone with passive-aggressive behaviors, I know they may be acting this way because I've hurt them. Today, I would try to pursue them by saying, "I feel I've hurt you. I'd love to fix what is going on. When you are ready, I'd love to hear what's really going on."

What I do not ask a passive-aggressive person is, "What's wrong?" I know I won't get a real answer. It's not right for me to tell someone else how to feel, so I don't want to tell them they are upset. I simply observe a behavior and address it. I observe that the behavior has changed, and I want to give you an opportunity to speak into it. By creating a safe place for a person to talk, I hope to overcome their fear and allow them to talk about what is truly wrong. I can't force them to talk, but I also can address unhealthy behavior. If someone is passive-aggressively attacking, that behavior has to be addressed. I do my best to not get upset by reminding myself that hurt people hurt people. Passive-aggressive behavior is a response to big feelings that the other person doesn't know how to deal with. By creating a safe place for them to talk, my goal is to help solve the problem.

The Aggressive Person!

The aggressive person needs to see that you are not weak. Don't fight back. You'll only enrage them more. Aggressive people are like the Incredible Hulk. You fight back and they only get more angry. You cannot let an aggressive person bully you or intimidate you.

Years ago there was a person that we contracted out to do some work for us. They continually failed to do what they said they were going to do. In fact, I caught them in multiple lies. Each time I tried to show grace and care. It finally got to a point where we had to make a change. When they were made aware of the change, they quickly shot off an e-mail attacking me. They said all sorts of things including calling me a liar. I responded back quickly with, "I've always tried to show you respect. I understand you're upset, but I will not talk to you until you can respect me." Within minutes he e-mailed and apologized. I'm not going to be pulled into a fight. When someone fights ugly, I want to respond with grace. But that doesn't mean I let them walk all over me.

When someone is aggressive, you can make your statement and then leave if you have to. Just don't let their unhealthy behavior bring you to an unhealthy place. An aggressive person may not even realize how they are coming across. They may be yelling to you, but in their mind, they think they are simply communicating. It's okay to communicate that you want respect. You do not need to accuse or attack them. Simply communicate, "I want to feel respected and I'm not feeling respected. When we can have a respectful conversation, I will gladly talk with you."

Paul Has More to Say

Look at what Paul says next:

> Do not be overcome by evil, but overcome evil with good. (Rom. 12:21)

These are such powerful words! When we respond to evil with evil, nobody wins. This is why we must learn to treat others how we want to be treated, not how we are feeling. When we allow someone's unhealthy behavior to cause us to react instead of respond, we lose. In the name of Jesus, let's be powerful people that overcomes evil with good. That includes our families, friendships, neighbors, and coworkers.

When conflict happens and we choose to respond instead of react, we give ourselves a chance to solve the problem. We often act as if the role of conflict is to win. We react in conflict in a way that attempts to hurt the other person. Please note that is the wrong goal of conflict.

The goal of conflict is to find the best possible answer.

All relationships have conflict. All. Every relationship has conflict. It has been estimated that the average couple argues 2,455 times a year. That ends up being roughly seven times a day. Whenever I do premarital counseling, I always do a session on conflict. Most couples when asked say they don't have much conflict in their relationship. That is a common response. Something is off with the amount of conflict we have and the amount of conflict we acknowledge. We don't like to think about or talk about conflict. We also want people to think we have better relationships than we actually do. So we are tempted to pretend like everything is great when in all actuality there is conflict. One of the biggest issues with conflicts in relationships is that we avoid it. This happens at jobs, in friendships, and at churches.

Sixty-nine percent of all conflicts are never solved.

The reason that conflicts are rarely solved is because we rarely allow someone else to work on the actual problem. When we react instead of respond, we rarely solve anything. We think that if we hurt them with passive, passive-aggressive, or aggressive behavior, we will win but in reality we lose. We lose a connection, and worst-case scenario, we lose the relationship.

Conflicts solve problems when we fight for our relationships instead of in our relationships.

The way to fight for my relationships is to become the healthiest person I can. As far as it depends on you, bring peace to every relationship. You cannot control what other people do, but for the good of your relationships, you must work on controlling yourself. You do this when you choose to respond instead of react to conflict.

You should not kill actual jerks. You cannot control other jerks. The best case we have is to identify the jerk inside us and make him obedient to Jesus. When we respond instead of react, we kill the jerk inside.

Chapter 7 is all about communication. Communication is so difficult in relationships, but we can get better at it. Before we jump to the next chapter, here are some questions for reflection.

The Win for this chapter: Think about a time where you have reacted instead of responding properly to a situation. Decide now how you will respond if a similar situation happens again.

Questions for Further Reflection

1. When conflict happens are you more passive, passive-aggressive, or aggressive? If you do not know, ask someone close to you. They know.
2. How can understanding how you react to conflict help you choose a better response?
3. Do you believe that you can choose to respond to conflict in a more healthy way? Why or why not?
4. How have you seen tit for tat or reacting to conflict hurt a relationship?
5. Based on this chapter, what is one thing you are going to do?

CHAPTER 7

How to Communicate What's Inside

You ever notice just how angry everyone is? We are an angry people. Now, I don't think of myself as an angry person. I think I'm pretty laid back. In fact, I would say that I am a peacemaker. In other words, I'm a lover, not a fighter. One thing I've learned about myself is that it's really difficult to see faults in myself. It's incredibly easy to see the faults in others, but it's very difficult to see the faults in yourself. So I am constantly looking for ways to better understand myself. In order to gain self-awareness I've taken a few of the personality tests out there. A couple of years ago I learned about the Enneagram test. I cannot recommend this high enough. I also greatly recommend reading the book *The Road Back to You*. I've gained great insight into myself and my relationships through Enneagram. The test was amazing. One section I particularly liked said, "Optimistic, reassuring, supportive: have a healing and calming influence—harmonizing groups, bringing people together: a good mediator, synthesizer, and communicator."

That is really good stuff, but it wasn't all good news. In the sections about relational issues it said, and I quote: "Suppression, control, and outbursts of temper—all of which are generally unrecognized and unacknowledged by the Nine."

Now this was some horribly good insight for me. At my best, I'm fun and peaceful, but at my worst I'm controlling with outbursts of temper that go unrecognized. So when there are things in my life like stress or especially relational tensions I will be at my worst. According to this personality test, I tend to suppress my feelings and then when it comes out it comes out in outbursts of temper. Up until this moment it used to baffle me when my wife, Monica, would ask, "Why are you so mad?" To which I almost always reply, "I'm not mad!" It happened when I was stressed, but what I learned is that the vast majority of the time when I felt stressed or upset, it was a result of a conflict in a relationship. Often a conflict in a relationship with someone else would come out in conflict with my wife. Because I'm not aware of my tone of anger, I would get defensive when my wife would ask me this. Since learning this about myself, I've tried to simply apologize to my wife. I then start to analyze and reflect on where my stress is coming from. Almost 100 percent of the time when I'm expressing anger it's not because of the situation in front of me. It's because there is a conflict unresolved somewhere else in my life. It may be work, friends, or someone from church; but the emotion of anger comes out at my family. Jerk!

Communicating why I feel what I feel is incredibly difficult to me. I can communicate anger, but like we saw in the last chapter, that's not helpful. I'm not alone in this. We are some angry people, and we live in an angry country. I don't know about you, but when I look around I feel everyone is angry at everything. There are protests against the people who protest.

Christians are called to a higher standard. Thousands of years ago the apostle Paul became one of the main leaders of the Christian faith. It was early in his lifetime, and Paul gives some instructions to Christians about how to be separate from the world. In the middle of this section, Paul writes, "In your anger do not sin" (Eph. 4:26a).

Now notice the first part of this verse is in quotes. If you want to unlock the Bible, you have to ask questions when you read it. Who is Paul quoting in this verse? That's a great question. Thank you for asking. In my Bible I have a little footnote at the bottom that says Paul is quoting Psalm 4:4 (see Septuagint). So let's go to Psalm 4:4 and see what Paul is quoting. Most of the psalms are written by another prime-time player of the Scriptures, David. Look at what David writes:

> Tremble and do not sin; when you are on your beds, search your hearts and be silent. (Ps. 4:4)

So Paul is quoting this, but it's not an exact quote. I'm a little confused. At the bottom of my Bible I have a little note that says, "Or in your anger (see Septuagint)." This is second time I've seen the word *Septuagint.* I would love to see this Septuagint, but I don't have a fat clue what it is. The first time I saw it I didn't think much of it, but now my Bible is forcing me to do some extra research. I'm starting to get a little angry because it keeps telling me to see the Septuagint and I don't have a fat clue what that is. I have a masters in divinity from seminary. I also have a ministry degree from the largest Christian university in the world. I also grew up in the church. How in the world do I not have a fat clue what the Septuagint is? I'm sure I've heard the term before and have just blocked it out because it's not something I reference—ever. Thankfully, we have Google. Thanks to Google I learn:

The Septuagint is a translation of the Hebrew Bible and some related texts into Koine Greek. As the primary Greek translation of the Old Testament, it is also called the Greek Old Testament.

Thanks, Google!

In comparing the New Testament quotations of the Hebrew Bible, it is clear that the Septuagint was often used. This is the result of the fact that by the late first century BC, and especially the first century AD, the Septuagint had "replaced" the Hebrew Bible as the Scriptures most people used. Since most people spoke and read Greek as their primary language and the Greek authorities strongly encouraged the use of Greek, the Septuagint became much more common than the Hebrew Old Testament.

So Paul is quoting from the Greek translation of the Hebrew from the Old Testament. So that explains why there is a difference in this quote. But what does David's original quote mean? According to one commentary who writes like a pirate:

> If ye be angry, and if ye think ye have cause to be angry; do not let your disaffection carry you to acts of rebellion against both God and your king. Consider the subject deeply before you attempt to act. Do nothing rashly; do not justify one evil act by another: sleep on the business; converse with your open heart upon your bed; consult your pillow. (Clarke's Commentary)

Argh! I love that! Consult your pillow. In other words, anger is such a strong emotion that you better make sure it's justified. David said search your heart and be silent. In other words, you might need to cool off before you do something you are going to regret. Examine your heart. We have to search ourselves to figure out the root of the anger.

Now this is so important because anger can be a substitute emotion. According to one psychologist, this means that sometimes people make themselves angry so that they don't have to feel pain. It could be consciously or unconsciously, but when someone feels pain, it often comes out as anger. People change their feelings of pain into anger because it feels better to be angry than it does to be in pain.

You might be angry because you are actually sad. You might be angry because you are under some stress. You might be angry because you are hungry. You might be angry because you aren't getting enough sleep. You might be angry because you are a control freak and cannot handle when someone does something different than you. There are so many potential reasons we might be angry. This is one of the main reasons it is so difficult to communicate our emotions in a healthy way. Often what we are feeling is not the source of our pain. The jerk comes to life when we aren't at our best. Sometimes the most holy thing you can do is take a nap or eat a healthy meal. If you find yourself being extra jerk like, then take a deep breath and ask what is the heart behind these feelings. Maybe the issue at hand is as easily fixed as getting some more sleep. It's often difficult to find the source of our anger because we lack the self-awareness necessary to figure it out.

A Rabbit Trail

For some, the jerk doesn't come out occasionally but regularly. I'm convinced if we were more self-aware we would be appalled at our jerk-like behavior. I recently read that only 13 percent of the population is self-aware. That's alarming!

Why is being self-aware important? It's important because it's an understanding of how we see and react to the world. If we are not self-aware, then we have little hope in changing.

Self-awareness is having a clear understanding of your personality. This includes strengths, weaknesses, beliefs, motives, and emotions. Self-awareness allows you to understand other people, how they perceive you, and how you respond to them.

So how can you improve self-awareness?

1. Respond instead of react to your emotions. Self-aware people do not stuff emotions, and they do not spill their emotions on others. They respond to the emotion by asking, "What am I feeling," and "Why am I feeling this way?"
2. Know your strengths. Self-aware people are confident in what they are gifted at.
3. Understand your weaknesses. Self-aware people know they have some weaknesses and that's okay. They don't have to be ashamed. We were created to need others, and when you understand your weakness, you can live from your strengths.
4. Seek feedback. We don't know what we don't know. Asking, "What's it like on the other side of me," is a tough but helpful question. Understanding

how others perceive you is a big part of becoming self-aware.

I'm still a work in progress; but for me, growing in my own self-awareness has helped me improve my marriage, friendships, and leadership. It also impacts my relationship with God. The more self-aware I become, the more clear it is that I need a Savior. I'm a jerk in need of Jesus. Thankfully, I'm better than I used to be but I'm not yet where I want to be. When we grow in self-awareness, it gives us a greater potential to see the inner jerk and in return put him in a body bag.

Now Back to Our Regularly Scheduled Chapters

Show me someone who is offended all the time, and I will show you someone who hasn't dealt with their feelings of pain and lacks self-awareness. Hurt people do indeed hurt people. When we do not deal with the root of the emotion, we respond in anger but often ignore the cause. The inner jerk thinks that we are angry at traffic, someone's Facebook post, only having three lines open at Walmart, kids, bosses, employees, neighbors, etc. You may be angry at one of those things, but the degree in which you experience the anger could be based on another source of pain in your life. You can tell if you are not consistent in your anger. For example, I never enjoy traffic. There are some times where I'm calm through traffic and there are other times when I want to call down fire from heaven on other drivers. Most of the time when my anger rises in traffic, it's because of something else going on in my life. Either I'm stressed because I left too late and I am going to be late to my destination, I'm hungry, I'm sleepy, or I have unresolved conflict with someone. What I've found to be true, more times than not, is that when everything is balanced in my life, I am way more gracious toward other drivers.

For me, when I'm stressed, I'm more prone to get angry. It's been true for my whole life, but I finally was able to put some words to it when I took the Enneagram test. I also become an emotional wreck when there is someone upset with me. I love bringing peace, and I hate conflict. Knowing someone I care about is upset with me hurts me deeply. I'm a work in progress. What I now know is that when I'm losing my temper it is almost always a result of some unresolved pain in my life.

Now Paul doesn't tell us how to "not sin" when we get angry. He just says, "In your anger do not sin." It's like he is trusting us to figure out what this means. Now that's not something we are very good at. We love for people to just tell us how to fix our problems. We like to solve our problems like following the steps to a recipe. To not sin in your anger, just add gluten-free, HMO-free, carb-free water. But it's not that easy because different things make different people angry. So what's it going to take for you not to sin in your anger?

The part you have to figure out is what makes you angry enough to sin.

Anger is an emotion like crying, or laughing, or being stressed. God gave us our emotions to work together and help us survive this world. But there are some things you can't handle with your anger. You are not wired to handle certain things, and if you put yourself in situations where you can't handle your anger, you will sin.

Sin is easier to avoid than resist.

If you put yourself in situations where you have to resist sin, you have a greater chance of falling. If you are on a diet and trying to avoid some unhealthy foods, don't have them in the house. The temptation is too great. In order to not sin in your anger, you have to know what triggers your anger. It means you have to figure out ways to cope with the things that make you angry in a healthy way. You've got to find what works for you. You might need to stay off social media. You might need to stop watching political news programs. You might need to see a Christian counselor to deal with the pain you have experienced. My friend told me one time that he has a hard time trusting people who don't drink alcohol. He said I'm one of the few he trusts. I feel that way about counseling. If you haven't talked to a pastor, psychologist, or professional counselor, I have a hard time trusting you've dealt with your issues. For some reason our culture has stigmatized counseling as something only crazy people need. I view counseling like I view a mechanic. Some people have spent their life learning how to fix the things that are broken. I don't want to wait until my car is broke down to have it looked at. I don't know a lot about cars, so I take my car for regular checkups at the mechanic. Counseling is the same way. I've gone to see a counselor multiple times in my life. I also read books that help me learn to be more self-aware and cope in stressful situations. I'm a work in progress, but if there is no learning, there is no progress. If you don't deal with that pain, the anger will come out somewhere.

Let's see what Paul says next:

> Do not let the sun go down while you are still angry. (Eph. 4:26b)

This is incredibly practical advice. Don't let the sun go down while you are still angry. This is a good rule. In fact, it's one of the rules my wife and I have for marriage. It's a great rule, but remember the idea behind what King David wrote? "Do nothing rashly; do not justify one evil act by another: sleep on the business; converse with your open heart upon your bed; consult your pillow."

The point of Paul's verse is not to give us a specific time frame, but to give us a warning. It is not healthy to react in strong emotions, and it is equally unhealthy to ignore strong emotions. We need some time to process what we are feeling, and then we need to intentionally deal with those feelings. Way too often our emotions are so strong we resort to burying them. Unresolved conflicts do not make the conflicts go away. In fact, a frustration is never content until it's expressed. This is why if after some time of reflecting, giving yourself some space, if you are still frustrated, then it's unhealthy to bury that emotion.

Twenty-four hours gives me enough time to cool down, and it gives me enough time for to process what's really going on. Sometimes I'm not really angry; I'm hangry (hungry + angry = hangry). Some of the time I'm not really frustrated; I'm tired. Sometimes I'm not really angry; I'm stressed. Sometimes my anger at others is really a result of something that I need to work on in myself.

In your anger do not sin, but also do not avoid issues. If you get to know someone, at some point you will get angry at them. Remember chapter 4 about unmet expectations? You may have thought you were done with it, but here it is again.

Mismanaging expectations leads to anger.

1. We mismanage when we do not communicate expectations.
2. We mismanage when we have unrealistic expectations.

The vast majority of the time our inner jerk comes out when our expectations have not been met. They are not met because either they are unspoken or unrealistic. Think about this. If you are driving down the interstate and a car cuts you off without putting on a blinker, it upsets you. Depending on how you respond to anger, it might be the reason you don't put a Christian magnet or bumper sticker on your car. You know yourself well enough that you know your road rage doesn't represent Jesus. I respect that. The point being in that moment, you and I become angry. We become angry because we expect other drivers to follow the rules of the road. When they don't meet our expectations, the immediate reaction is anger. Depending on what else is going on in our life will depend on what degree of anger we respond with. Because anger is a secondary emotion, your anger could vary between a Christian substitute curse word and the real deal.

Learning to Communicate Our Emotions

Strong emotions are difficult to communicate. A way to help with expressing your inner feelings is to…

Big Idea: Manage your anger by communicating your expectations, feelings, and emotions in healthy ways.

Now, why is what Paul wrote so important? Because if you don't take care of the little things that make you angry day by day, you will store a list of offenses in your brain. Eventually, that list will come out on the other person. Have you ever experienced the list?

Years ago, there was a relationship that was off in my life. This person started avoiding me, and we no longer hung out like we used to. I do not like confrontation, but I love people, so when there is an issue, I address it. I wanted to figure out what was going on, so I confronted the situation by saying, "I feel like there is something going on, but I don't know what it is. I care about you and our relationship, so I want to work on whatever is going on." At this point this person unloaded the list on me. The list is a plethora of wrongs that have been compiled. There were offenses on the list that I had no idea about. Some of the offenses were over a year old, and at that point there was nothing I could do to fix the relationship. The list was too long and had been held on to for too long. If you are married or have ever been married, you may have experienced the list. You've felt something was off in the relationship, and when you opened the door, the list came pouring out. Things like, "You never clean up after yourself," "I have to tell you forty-eight times to take out the trash," "You compliment other people's cooking, but never compliment mine," "You never notice all the things I do." The list. Friends can have a list, parents, coworkers, etc. The list is when someone holds on to offenses. This could be a result of being a stuffer. It's understandable why someone might have a hard time addressing offenses, but it's an unhealthy move in relationships.

If you are carrying a list of wrongs caused by someone close to you, you are in the wrong.

Now that doesn't mean that what they did was okay. It doesn't mean that they didn't have a part to play. But people can't read your mind. People don't know your expectations. And way too many relationships come to end because of a list of wrongs. By the time the list comes out, it is too late. It's too difficult to go back. So Paul says, before the sun goes down on your anger, you've got to deal with the issue at hand. If we don't deal with the root of the anger, we open ourselves up to some real danger. Look at what Paul says next.

The Devil's Foothold

> Do not give the devil a foothold. (Eph. 4:27)

How does Satan get a foothold? One offense at a time. At some point you may have had a relationship go from good to bad. You have people in your life who you used to be close with but are no longer close with. Or maybe you had someone who you were so in love with and now you can't stand them. Whether it is someone moving further away from you or you moving further away from someone else, at some point we experience heartbreak by the loss of a relationship. As a pastor let me give you some insight into the church world. The vast majority of the time when someone says, "I'm not longer being fed by my pastor's preaching," there is an offense that is not being dealt with. It's easier to say the pastor isn't feeding me than it is to deal with the offense. It becomes next to impossible to hear from God when you are offended by the preacher. Preachers are not perfect. If you truly care about someone, even the preacher, you'll have a healthy conversation. Way too many people leave churches under the guise of not being fed when the truth is they are offended. They didn't get asked to do something, they were overlooked, their needs weren't met, or they disagreed. Now there are some exceptions to this, but in my experience, when a person is no longer feeling fed, the vast majority of the time it started with an offense.

Satan wants nothing more than to destroy you. And if he can keep you distracted with a list of offenses, then you won't have time to do things for God's kingdom. God blesses us by putting people in our lives. The enemy distracts us by trying to separate us from the very people God has placed in our life. The enemy knows that we are better together. He knows it so well because he lives it. You ever notice how in the verses we read about the devil in Scripture, he is always unified with evil spirits. We never see two demons fighting with each other. If you are going through difficulty and your first thought is to pull away from people that can help you, please know that is not from God. God uses people to bless us. The enemy knows we can be picked off when we are isolated and alone. The enemy knows that if he can get us distracted with fighting each other we will be too exhausted to change the world.

We can't do life alone.

> For our struggle is not against flesh and blood, but against the rulers, against the authorities, against the powers of this dark world and against the spiritual forces of evil in the heavenly realms. (Eph. 6:12)

When we hold on to anger, resentment, and bitterness, we will at some point over communicate. At that point the person listening will more than likely miss the real reason we are upset. That's why waiting until you calm down is healthy, but waiting too long is unhealthy. Deal with anger in a healthy way by communicating it within twenty-four hours. It's been often said, "Holding on to bitterness is like drinking poison and expecting the other person to die." It may feel natural to hold on to your anger, but it's killing you.

How to Communicate What You Are Feeling

Once you are at a healthy place to communicate, the next step is to understand how to communicate. Often, when we are frustrated, we lash out by telling the other person what they've done. See if you can relate to the following.

You had the expectation that you were going to have a nice night out with someone you love. You've been looking forward to this for some time. On the day of the hangout this loved one bails on you. They give some lame excuse, but the truth is they are not prioritizing your relationship. You've forgiven them before, but this time it's the final straw. This time you are going to tell them how you feel. It goes something like this:

"You always cancel on me. You don't value the relationship like I do. I don't understand *why you don't care about me as much as I do you*!" Note that this conversation often uses caps lock and lots of exclamation points.

Now, reread that last three sentences in quotes. You went to tell them how you were feeling, but you didn't communicate what you were feeling. You communicated what you believe is wrong with them. At this point the other person will become defensive. Depending on how they handle conflict, they will either become passive, passive-aggressive, or aggressive. They may say, "Sorry," but it's safe to say they are thinking you are a jerk. Accusing someone will only put them on the defense. It is unsafe to tell others how they feel. It is unsafe to tell others what their motives are. Lack of communication destroys relationships because instead of knowing how the other person is feeling, we make assumptions. When we do not know the whole story, we complete the narrative in our mind, and most of the time isn't unhelpful and missing some details. This is wrong! It is unfair to assume you know why someone did what they did. The key is to express what you are feeling without accusing them. We do this by using "I" statements.

I vs. You Statements

The key to expressing how you feel in a healthy way is to use "I" statements. Now, this is not easy. It's not easy because we often don't know why we feel how we feel. That's where you need some time to process and consult your pillow. This is where becoming self-aware comes in. You need some time to think about how you are feeling. Do not spend this time thinking about how wrong or evil the other person is. That is not helpful. What can be helpful is learning to communicate what is going on inside of you.

We know what we feel. We feel emotions. We feel anger, excitement, joy, sorrow. We often struggle to know why we feel how we feel.

This is why many of the conflicts we get into never get solved. We end up fighting about things that are not the real issue. When you do the hard work to know why you are feeling and what you are feeling, you can respond instead of react to conflict.

Years ago, my wife, Monica, was not feeling connected to me. I was busy with work and had unintentionally not prioritized her. She was feeling more like a roommate than a soul mate. I was a very good roommate. I clean up after myself, put the toilet seat down, and am somewhat low maintenance. Monica was needing a connection. In her attempt to communicate with me, she did exactly what she was hoping I would do for her. She put me first. She prioritized me. She went out of her way to make me feel special. During this week she bought me surprise gifts, made favorite meals, and even drove one hour to my favorite restaurant and then back to deliver me lunch. This was full of awesome! I was thankful but clueless. At the end of the week Monica communicated what she was feeling, and then it all clicked. She said, "I'm not feeling connected. I kept doing nice things to try to get your attention. I'd love to feel prioritized. I want to feel like your soul mate and not a roommate."

That response did not make me defensive in the least. She didn't tell me I was a horrible husband. She didn't tell me I was clueless to her kindness. She didn't tell me what was wrong with me. She did not say, "You don't love me like I love you!" She communicated what was going on inside of her. When we feel hurt, we often assume the other person did it on purpose and then we explain to them the reason why.

It is a jerk move to tell someone else how they feel. It's a jerk move to tell someone why they did what they did. By nature, we assume the worst about others. It's called fundamental attribution error, and it's the belief that when a person does something wrong, it is because they are defective. When we are hurt, we naturally believe that there is something wrong with the other person. The issue is when we do the same thing, we believe it is for a good reason. So if someone doesn't return your phone call, you say, "They are so selfish. All they care about is themselves." But when you fail to call someone back, you say, "I've just been extra busy." You see, we attack others while we often give ourselves the benefit of the doubt.

"I" statements are powerful and effective. The inner jerk wants to come out when you've been hurt, and he loves to point out the flaws of the other person. That's not helpful. Instead practice communicating "I" statements. The emotions we feel can be so strong we will communicate in an unhealthy way, and in return the issue will not be resolved. Instead, practice thinking about what's really going on inside of you and communicate that by using an "I" statement.

Try This, Not That

Here are some examples of common things we say in frustration and examples of what we could say instead:

You statement: You are always late! You just don't care about me.
I statement: I'm not feeling respected, and being on time communicates respect to me.

You statement: You are so selfish! All you do is think about yourself.
I statement: I'm not feeling valued, and I want to feel valued. When you think of me, it shows me value.

You statement: You always leave your underwear on the floor. You're such a slob!

I statement: I'm feeling stressed by the mess, and I'd like to feel relaxed. When I have to clean up after others, I don't feel relaxed.

You statement: Why are you so mean?
I statement: I feel uncomfortable when you raise your voice to me.

You statement: You are so lazy!
I statement: I feel like there is more in you. I believe in you and your potential to do more.

Now it's your turn. Practice by filling in the blank with some potential "I" statements.

You statement: You are so sensitive!
I statement: ________________.

You statement: You should know better than doing something that stupid!
I statement: ________________.

You statement: You make me so angry!
I statement: ________________.

You statement: You never listen to me!
I statement: ________________.

I statements are so important. After all, we are to treat others how we would want to be treated, not how we are feeling. This may feel daunting to start practicing. Maybe no one has ever demonstrated healthy relationships to you.

Don't you wish someone did? You can be that person for someone else.

I Have a Strong Feeling This Is the End of the Chapter

It is. It is the end of the chapter.

This chapter's Win: Manage your anger by communicating your expectations, feelings, and emotions by using "I" statements.

Questions for Further Reflection

1. What emotion do you struggle to express the most?
2. Did you skip over the practicing "I" statements?
3. What will it take for you to go back and practice the "I" statements?
4. I feel there is more in you and you are better than skipping practicing the "I" statements. Now it's your turn.
5. What is your biggest takeaway from this chapter?
6. What are you going to do about that takeaway?

CHAPTER 8

Jerks Don't Know How to Fight

Communication is one of the pillars for any healthy relationship. Too bad most of us stink at it. We may not think we stink at it, but we do. The more we communicate in healthy ways, the less conflict we will have. The less we communicate, the more conflict we have.

Communicating is difficult because we often get in our own way. I don't know about you, but often I communicate best when it's just me having an internal conversation with someone I disagree with. I am like the lawyer Johnnie Cochran in his prime in my own mind. I have the best arguments, the quickest comebacks, and I'm always right. Then I get around someone I disagree with in person, I become Chewbacca from Star Wars. Words come out, but no one seems to have a fat clue what I'm saying. I try getting louder, and that doesn't help. I end up over communicating, and when that happens, I tend to have to apologize.

That is until I learned the goal of communication.

Big Idea: The goal of communication is understanding not agreeing.[4]

I'll get to that in a few moments, but for now I want you to think about this question.

What will it take to become great at this relationship?

Think about a relationship that you have difficulty with. Think about a relationship where you struggle to see eye to eye. Most likely, if you have answers for what it will take to become great at the relationship, most of them involve the other person changing. That's not going to cut it here. We cannot change other people. We can only work on changing and controlling ourselves. With that being said, what will it take for you to become great at this relationship?

Take a few moments to think about the question. You don't have to have a lot of answers. I find that working on oneself instead of focusing on others issues helps keep the jerk at bay. Before you move on to the next section, spend a few moments simply thinking about what it will take to become great at this relationship.

The Foundation for This Chapter

I'm so thankful for Scripture. The Scripture for this entire chapter gives us amazing direction at how to become great at relationships. The Scripture was written by Jesus's brother. His name was James. His writing is very practical,

---

4 My understanding of this was greatly enlightened by a teaching I heard from Danny Silk.

to the point, and easy to understand. James gives us some amazing insight into how to have healthy relationships. I'll show you what he says, and then we will go on an adventure together. What follows is not easy to live out, but it's so powerful. James writes:

> Everyone should be quick to listen, slow to speak and slow to become angry, because human anger does not produce the righteousness that God desires. (James 1:19–20)

Before you read the next section, would you take a moment to pray and ask God to speak to your heart? You don't have to do this, but I find I often get in my own way. God speaks often, but I often miss it because of my distractions, faulty opinions, or laziness. Communication is such a big deal to relationships, and I'm convinced that healthy communication with God helps us have better communication with people. If you are willing, spend a few seconds praying. If you don't know what to pray, I recommend the following: "God, speak to my heart and give the courage to obey you even when it's hard."

The Communication Adventure Begins

One day a lady in a brand-new BMW had been driving around a crowded store parking lot. There was no parking, and she had circled the lot multiple times. Then, like a modern-day miracle, she sees a car leave. She puts her blinker on and decides to back into the spot. The parking lot is so busy, she knows backing in now will make exiting easier when she leaves. Right as she started to back in, a young guy driving a supped-up muscle car whizzed into the spot before her. As the young driver got out of his car, the woman in the BMW rolled down her window to let him have it. She declared, "That was my spot! You saw I was backing into it. What gives you the right take it?" The young man laughed and said, "Because I'm young and quick so there's that!" and then kept on walking. His smile quickly turned to a fearful look when he heard a loud crash. He turned around to see the lady in the BMW repeatedly slamming her car into his. He was obviously upset and yelled at the woman, "Are you crazy! Why would you do something like this?" The woman quickly said, "Because I'm old and I'm rich so there's that."

In so many ways I think all of us can relate to that story. The story is fictitious, but it represents what happens when we disagree with others. When someone disagrees with us, we react. If they don't change their opinion, we react some more, but this time it's usually louder. Damage is done, but we don't feel too bad about it because they deserved it. The problem of going back and forth like this rarely solves any issues. In fact, so many of our issues rarely get solved. We fight. We argue. We ignore certain subjects because they just never get solved.

There is a better way. It involves becoming great at communication. According to psychologists, one of the leading building blocks for a healthy relationship is communication. Whether it's family, neighbors, friends, or coworkers, communication is crucial. It's foundational to having and maintaining healthy relationships.

The definition of healthy communication is very different than what I think of when I think about communication. Communication means a lot of different things to a lot of different people, but effective communication is more than talking.

Effective communication involves the ability to pay attention to what others are thinking and feeling.

Now that is a very different definition from what we do. For most people, communicating is talking and reacting to what others are saying. A lot of our communication is two people taking turns talking. Effective communication is more than simply exchanging words. Effective communication involves paying attention to what others are thinking and feeling. I love the quote: "The single biggest problem in *communication* is the illusion that it has taken place" (George Bernard Shaw).

Most people stink at communication. We talk, someone responds, and then we talk some more. This continues until we have nothing left to say or it's time to leave. Let's revisit the question I started this chapter with:

What will it take for you to become great at this relationship?

The answer: communication.

I want to show you practically how you can do this. Let's look at what James says.

> Everyone should be quick to listen, slow to speak and slow to become angry. (James 1:19)

Now this is great advice for everyone, but in this case everyone doesn't mean every one. James is writing to

Christians. We are going to see in a few moments why that is important. If you are reading this as a Christian, then this applies to you. I think this is such great advice everyone should apply, but we will see why this is so important for Christians when we get to the end of the verse. Every Christian should be quick to listen, slow to speak, and slow to become angry. You will not agree with what everyone in your family says. You will not agree with every decision a leader makes. You cannot control other people, but as a Christian, God gives you the power to control yourself.

So when you communicate, you should be quick to listen, slow to speak, and slow to become angry. The question is why don't we do that? We do not communicate very well because we've never learned how to and very few people have modeled it for us. I communicate for a living, and it is so much easier to communicate when I have a captive audience. It's taken me years of research, counseling, and practice to be a better communicator one on one, especially when emotions get involved. I tend to be more aggressive when my feelings get involved. At the same time I hate conflict, so in order to not be aggressive I shut down. I don't want to be aggressive, and I do not want to shut down. This is where being quick to listen comes in.

Listen, Listen, Listen

When we communicate, we rarely listen. Research shows that the average person only remembers 17–25 percent of the information they hear. If that's the case, why aren't we taking better notes? We tell ourselves we will remember, but we don't. We listen, but we rarely hear. I can attest to this every time my wife asks me to pick up something from the store. I get to the store, and I don't have a fat clue what my wife asked me to get. If I don't write it down when she says it, I'll end up going to the store and buying stuff she didn't ask for, all the while forgetting to buy what she did ask for. Jerk!

There are two things that are helpful for listening. The first is repeating back what is being said. If you are listening to a sermon, reading a book, or taking in information where you cannot repeat it out loud, then taking notes by writing down what is said does the same thing. A second thing that is helpful in listening is to find something to fidget with. This is based on research and not just for people with ADD. In my office I have Thinking Putty, so whenever I am in a meeting and need to listen, I bring it out. If I don't have Thinking Putty, I take notes. Sometimes I draw 3D boxes on the notes. There are extremes to this where the item you use to fidget takes away your ability to listen, but something small can actually help your brain focus. Research shows having something to fidget with can help to focus, and I have found it helps me not get distracted. Listening is hard work. It's even harder for those of us that are men.

When it comes to listening, men only use half their brains where as women use both sides of their brains. So if you are a woman and you are wondering if a guy is listening just know it's a 50/50 chance.

I once heard a joke that said, "My wife fussed at me and said, 'You weren't listening to me!' I thought, *That's a weird way to start a conversation*."

Some men may not like what I'm about to write. I think it's helpful, so I'm going to share it. The next time you are wondering if a man is listening or not, ask him to repeat back the last thing you said. Don't get mad. Don't yell or insult him. Just ask him? If he can't remember, then he will have to come clean. And if you continually do this, you'll help reinforce good listening habits. This is also a helpful technique in meetings. To wrap up a meeting, ask those involved, "What did you hear?" To close a lot of meetings I'll include a recap of everyone's assignments. It's a quick recap to make sure everyone is on the same page. I also do this with my kids. Often I will ask them to repeat what they heard me say. The single biggest problem in communication is assuming that it's taken place. Do not assume.

Let's be honest, when it comes to communication, everyone needs a little help. It's not just the men. One of the issues with communication is how we use so much more than words to communicate.

Your words only convey about 7 percent of what you're trying to say. The other 93 percent is communicated through facial expressions and the tone of your voice.

This is why we have to be quick to listen! By nature, we stink at listening, and based on that stat we stink at communicating. No wonder there are so many communication issues in relationships. We think we are being clear when we communicate, but we are often expecting people to pick up on clues we leave as we say very little. The truth is, no one can read your mind. If you want others to know what's going on with you, it takes learning to communicate what's going on inside of you. If you do not communicate what's inside of you, then the other person will more than likely complete the part of the story they don't know. They will assume something about you, and most of the time that assumption is wrong. Talking, communicating, and asking questions helps to unearth what is truly going on inside of us. That takes us back to James. Let's focus on the first word James mentioned:

listening. There are two types of listening. There is listening and active listening.

Active listening is a skill that can be developed. Active listening involves your whole senses. It is difficult to actively listen and multitask. It's difficult to actively listen and be glued to your smartphone. So much of communication involves facial expressions and the tone of voice that we must be fully present in order to become great at listening. Now this at first may seem like it goes against what I wrote about fidgeting. The difference is, in fidgeting your brain doesn't have to process new information. In multitasking, we are asking our brains to focus on two things at once. When we do that, we miss out on some of the information.

Writing about listening (I would say speaking about listening, but you are reading and I am writing) a good rule of thumb is to communicate important information in person instead of in text. E-mail, text, and social media are difficult to convey tone. I know we have moved away from phone calls and in many cases face-to-face conversations, but if it's important it should be done in person. Save text for inconsequential information or facts. Examples include, "What time is dinner?" "Don't forget to pick up ice cream at the grocery store on your way home from work." "Did you watch the game last night?" Memes. Memes are hilarious and for the most part great to share via text or social media. Way too often disagreements are escalated because important information was communicated via text. What is not helpful is to try and solve a conflict via text. So much of communication is body language and tone, and it's impossible to convey that over text. The Scriptures say,

> If one gives an answer before he hears, it
> is his folly and shame. (Prov. 18:13)

Put that in your pipe and smoke it. Or if you are a Baptist, put that in your potluck and eat it. If I had a $1 for every time I spoke before I truly heard what someone said, I'd be filthy rich.

Very few people are good at listening. In fact, you may not be listening right now. Our brains are wired to zone out. Have you ever driven somewhere while your brain was on autopilot? In seminary I would read whole books and not have a fat clue what I read. The assignment was often to read hundreds of pages, and I read, but I didn't take in the information. Now when I read to learn, I underline, highlight, or make notes on the parts that stand out. If I don't participate in the reading, I often zone out and miss the information.

Active listening is more than just sitting still. It's observing, caring, leaning in, and asking follow-up questions. Active listening is observing as we listen.

When greeting someone, it is pretty standard for me to ask, "How are you doing?" Most of the time the reply back is, "I'm good," or something cliché like, "Can't complain." Often though someone will slip in an "Okay." Not a Lil John or Cardi B type of "Okay!"[5] It's more of a somber "Okay." Being an active listener means paying attention. So when I hear a somber "Okay," I ask, "Just okay?" Often I learn a lot about a current struggle the person is facing. It takes time and often takes away from what is on my schedule, but people are important and worth it. We show others they matter when we actively listen.

Active listening shows you care. In one of the small groups I led, I noticed one of the members was unusually quiet. I didn't want to call them out or embarrass them, so

[5] If you do not get this reference, please ask someone younger than you who also listens to rap music.

I waited until after-group. I mentioned to them something I observed. Observation is key to active listening. Observe and then share what you observe to see if you are right. It's not calling out or trying to embarrass. It's showing you care. This is a powerful tool in active listening. I shared with him, "I observed that you were more quiet this week than normal. Is everything okay?" Everything wasn't okay. He was dealing with some major stress and family drama. We were able to set up a time to grab coffee so we could talk.

Now granted you may not care about how most people are doing. That's fair. There are, however, people in your life; and they need to see they matter to you. Whether it's your kids, parents, siblings, spouse, friends, neighbors, coworkers, or roommate, there is someone in your life that needs to know you care. We are great at actively listening when we first meet someone we care about. We pay attention and are naturally on our best behavior during the honeymoon phase. Once the honeymoon phase ends, we have to be intentional with our listening or we will communicate we don't really care.

In order to become great at active listening, we have to practice. We have to learn to ask follow-up questions. We have to learn to ask clarifying questions. We have to care about the people in our lives and not just ourselves. We have to put away our smartphones and make eye contact. The first thing James tell us is to be quick to listen. He's not done. James then says to be slow to speak.

Slow to Speak (Said in a Sloth's Voice)

In order to learn to be slow to speak we must first seek to understand. Part of the issue is we listen for agreement. When we agree with someone, it often draws us in. We love having conversations with people who are just like us. We also hate dealing with disagreements. Nothing makes us speak faster than hearing something we disagree with.

We have believed a *lie* that we have to agree to be friends. *Truth: We can disagree and still be friends.*

This is especially important in relationships with the people closest to us. Often the biggest disagreements between friends, couples, and coworkers come down to a lack of understanding. We like people that are like us and attack those who are not.

The goal of communication is understanding not agreeing.

We listen for agreement, and then when we find disagreement, it engages us but for all the wrong reasons. Be quick to listen, and then when disagreement happens—and it will happen in all relationships—be slow to speak.

I don't have to agree with you. In order to have a healthy relationship, I must seek to understand where you are coming from. James says, "Be slow to speak." In order to do this, we need to learn why disagreements divide us.

Disagreements Lead to a Divide

Read the comments on almost any political post, and you'll see the divide that disagreement causes. When someone disagrees with us, we hate it. Why? Because agreement is wired to our identity. When we hear that someone disagrees with us, subconsciously it makes us doubt our own security. We feel safe with those who agree because we see they are like us. Differences divide. As humans we are wired to want to belong, so we naturally gather in tribes of people that agree. Coke or Pepsi, Duke or UNC, Republican or Democrat, cats or dogs, pineapple on pizza or you are a psychopath for putting pineapple on pizza, and church denominations are all examples of how we gather with those we agree with. I like Coke, but I prefer the taste of Pepsi. I cannot tell you how many times I've been told I was wrong for having this opinion. People are passionate about soda. These same people want me to choose. I've never met a full-calorie caffeinated soda I didn't like. I like Pepsi and Coke. Don't message me about this. I don't have to choose. Oh, and I also like pineapple on pizza. Please don't miss the point. When there is division, there is a natural divide. If we are not intentional, we will allow the divide to negatively impact the relationship.

So the natural reaction to a disagreement is to disregard the other person. Because if they are right and I am wrong, then there is something wrong with me. But if they are wrong, there must be something wrong with them. This is so jacked up! Depending on the disagreement and how ingrained it is to our identity, we will naturally dismiss others that are different.

It's easy to allow a disagreement to become heated because deep inside a disagreement feels like a rejection. So when we hear disagreement, we react because a part of us is feeling attacked. In order to protect ourselves, we argue to try to convince the other person that who we are is right. When they won't submit to our opinion, we ramp up our efforts. When we no longer feel safe, the jerk comes out to fight. Disagreement doesn't feel safe. It feels out of our control. When we feel out of control, we go to unhealthy methods to try and control others. This is where we fight unfair, yell, manipulate, shut down, bring up the past, name call, etc.

This where we need some agreed-upon rules of engagement. Remember those from chapter 5? Without those a disagreement leads to division, and it's often unhealthy. After we have failed to force the other person to submit to our way of thinking, we naturally begin to write the other person off. When the disagreement continues, we naturally start to reject the other person because we already feel rejected.

There is a process for disagreement. It's a process you may not have known you've gone through, but you have experienced it nonetheless. The process is, *disagreement leads to a divide and then disdain.*

Don't skip over that last sentence too quickly. I've seen way too many relationships become irreconcilable because of a disagreement. Disagreement leads to a divide and then disdain. Whenever we feel a disagreement, there immediately is a divide in our connection. If we do not do something to bridge this divide, we will end up having a disdain for the person we disagree with.

The Power of Disagreeing

When we disagree with someone, there is instantly a divide. Unless we are intentional, we will push away anyone who doesn't think just like us. I'm convinced this is why so many Americans are better friends with their political TV and radio shows than the actual people in their life. We feel safe hearing information that we already agree with. But we don't do chores with, pay bills with, go to church with, and or live life with people that always agree with us.

You can be right and still be wrong. The jerk doesn't believe this, but it's true. You can be right about a belief and be wrong in how you react to others who disagree. Having a right belief and then turning everyone who disagrees into a villain is wrong. It's wrong because at some point we all disagree. It's lonely always being right.

There is another way. You have to decide what is most important to you: being right or having healthy relationships. We can disagree and still be friends. The goal of communication is understanding, not agreeing. We cannot find a compromise as long as we view those that disagree as villains.

Now, if the goal of communication is agreement, then when we disagree, I will be quick to speak. But if the goal of communication is understanding, then I will be slow to speak. Being slow to speak is not saying don't talk at all. It's saying when there is a disagreement, I need more information. Without this information, I will naturally complete the story in my mind. I will make assumptions as to why someone did something to hurt me, and those assumptions will not believe the best about them.

Slow to Speak Gets the Prize

If listening is more than just hearing words, I must commit to getting to the heart of what others are saying. A few years ago my son was having a full-blown meltdown one morning. I couldn't figure out what was going on. He was mad about everything. I told him he could not talk to me disrespectfully and that he needed to sit in his room until he could talk to me with respect. I left, and after ten minutes I went to check on him to see if he was ready to talk with respect. He respectfully said, "No." He was not ready, so I gave him more time. When I came back the next time, he was ready to talk. He was feeling insecure about a shirt that he was supposed to wear at school. He had convinced himself that people would make fun of him. Instead of communicating what he was feeling, he reacted in anger. It's my job to figure out what is really going on, and I can do that with active listening. If I simply reacted to his bad behavior, I would not have been able to get to the heart of his hurt. We ended up having an amazing conversation about insecurity and where our ultimate security comes from. He ended up wearing the shirt because he felt confident after we talked.

So much of our communication issues stems from our inability to talk about what is really going on. We have to get better at this. To be unclear is to be unkind.

When we passively communicate what's going on, we are in the wrong. When we passive-aggressively communicate, we are in the wrong. When we aggressively communicate, we rarely communicate what the actual issue is and therefore we are in the wrong.

Now we all have to work on becoming better at communicating what's inside of ourselves. That's why I spent a whole chapter on learning how to do just that. It's not easy, so many will not do the hard work to have a healthy relationship. Many will settle for drama-filled, unsafe relationships because it's easier to pretend to be happy than it is to do the hard work to actually have happy relationships. When we are willing to work on ourselves, we can have healthy relationships. Here is the key to being slow to speaking:

In order to be slow to speak you must seek to find more information.

Every personality is different. Every person is different. It's unfair to expect others to react the same way you do to every situation. Because we do not understand, the natural reaction is to jump to a judgment that the other person is wrong for feeling something that you don't feel. When this happens, we are rarely slow to speak.

Here is what being slow to speak does not look like.

Signs that you are quick to speak:

- Telling others how they should feel
- Dismissing someone else's feelings
- Arguing before asking questions
- Making a judgment before you have all the facts

It is wrong to tell someone else how they should feel. Think about it for a second. When you are upset, has it ever helped you to hear, "You just need to calm down!" My guess is that hasn't helped. It also hasn't helped when someone tells you, "You shouldn't worry about that," "That's a silly thing to be afraid of," "Stop being so emotional." When you are dealing with a big emotion, the thing you crave is understanding. We desire empathy but often give judgment. You want someone to say, "That's difficult." Telling others how they should feel is communicating that you are the only important person in the relationship. As long as everyone feels the same as you do, then we are good to go. We don't live with people who are just like us, so we must learn how to understand. When we seek to understand, we are treating others like we wish to be treated.

The goal of communication is understanding, not agreeing.

I don't have to agree with what you say. In order to communicate well, I have to seek to understand what you are saying. Telling someone "not to be afraid" or "you shouldn't worry about that" does not help. Fighting harder to get someone to agree with you doesn't work.

It's not our place to tell others how they should feel. When we dismiss other's feelings, we communicate that we are the only person that matters in the relationship. Healthy relationships seek to understand each other instead of control one another.

Agreement is so ingrained in me that I often have to tell myself the same phrase. I know the goal of communication is understanding, not agreeing, and yet I often forget what I know. To help I say a phrase. You are welcome to borrow this. It has helped jerks like me.

The next time you are frustrated in a disagreement tell yourself, "I don't have all the information."

It may not seem like it's a powerful phrase, but I'm telling you it's a swift kick to the jerk. I don't have all the information.

Try it.

I'd encourage you to write it down somewhere. The next time you get on social media and see a post that makes you want to lose your testimony say out loud, "I don't have all the information." The next time someone you know says something that seems 100 percent wrong tell yourself, "I don't have all the information."

Why is this sentence so powerful? Because it helps us be slow to speak. Sometimes more information will help me see that my first reaction was wrong. Sometimes more information will help me understand where a person is coming from. Sometimes more information will simply help you not say something you'll regret later.

We do not have to agree. We must seek to understand if we want healthy relationships.

Push Back!

At this point I always, and I mean always, get push back on this idea. The pushback is, "What if the person is truly wrong?" What if a coworker, friend, church member, or someone on social media is truly wrong? The fear is that if we do not adamantly disagree and call them out, then we are showing we agree.

This is where empathy comes in. When I show understanding and empathy, I communicate that the other person matters. When we show empathy, we have a greater chance for the other person to actually hear us in our disagreement. Empathy does not mean I agree. It shows I care.

I've learned this the hard way. There have been times I've argued passionately and put my opinion over the relationship. Whether it was sports, whether *Die Hard* is a Christmas movie or not, or whether a quesadilla is a Mexican sandwich, I've pushed too hard to try and make people agree with me. When I first planted the church I pastor, I believed I could work with anyone. I love people, and I am wired to work with a team. Throughout my ministry career, I was a peacemaker on staffs and found friends in almost every personality type. I believed that with enough conversation I could learn to work with anyone. Then I planted a church.

Relationships weren't as easy as the lead pastor. I quickly found out that the pastor's whisper is a yell. What that means is, when I said things in a normal tone, they weighed more now that I was the pastor. I was used to speaking freely as a church staff member. People generally liked my ideas and liked working with me. All of a sudden, as a lead pastor, things changed. One of the biggest issues was my inability to understand when others disagreed. I couldn't understand why people would get so upset when we disagreed. I wasn't mean. I didn't yell—for the most part. More on this in the next paragraph. I often thought "I'm nice! Why are people so angry at me?" I'll tell you why. I did a horrible job of understanding where others were coming from when I disagreed with them!

One of our staff was especially puzzling to me. We had a great relationship outside of work, but at work we were often on two different pages. For example, one Sunday our toilets stopped working. All of them. We had three services, hundreds of people, and not one working toilet. Not in the kids area. Not for the adults. This is a major problem. Even though our services don't last more than an hour that's a long time to hold it. On Monday I brought it up in our staff meeting. I wasn't blaming anyone, and I wasn't upset. I was direct. This was a major problem that we needed to fix before the following Sunday. I asked if anyone had any ideas or knew of anything we should do. No one had any ideas, so I said to one of the staff members, "I need you to call a plumber and get them here as quickly as possible." I thought it was a reasonable request. The response I received back was shocking and unexpected.

With an upset tone I was told, "That's not my job! I won't do that." I didn't know how to reply to that. I could tell something was going on. The biggest issue I had in the response was I would never tell my boss that I wouldn't do something. That goes back to expectations. I became frustrated because I expect staff to do what they are told to do. I don't feel like I rule with an iron fist. If anything, it's a velvet hammer. I didn't think my request was unreasonable, but because this person didn't meet my expectation, I was frustrated. That's typically the heart of why we don't understand someone. They do things differently than we do. I paused, gathered my thoughts, and then said, "You and I can talk after this meeting. Let's keep going with the rest of the meeting." I stayed calm, but I was frustrated. Really frustrated!

After the meeting we went to my office to talk. I asked what was going on, and I was told, "Everyone dumps everything they don't want to do on me! Calling the plumber is not on my job description." I thought, *That's it! This bad attitude has gone on too long.* I passionately said back, "That's not true! We are a small staff, and we all do things we don't want to do! I'm the lead pastor of the church, and I just drained the baptistery. Is that on my job description?" I didn't wait for her to answer. "It's not," I boldly proclaimed. I then passionately communicated how we all do things we don't want to do. I let her know that I cared about her. In fact, I shared with her that if I didn't care about her so much I'd fire her. Jerk move on my part. In some strange way I was trying to communicate that I cared for this staff member. I was trying to say that I cared so much I've extended grace into a situation that I would not normally extend grace. I communicated horribly. Remember, the pastor's whisper is a yell. What this staff member heard was, "Rob wants to fire me." From there we continued talking.

I calmed down, and we ended on what I thought was a good note and understanding. I didn't know how to communicate when we disagreed. This staff member gave a letter of resignation the following week.

A little over a year later I was on an airplane flying to Israel. I brought the book *Keep Your Love On* by Danny Silk. It was given to me by someone at church. I receive lots of books, and most of the time they end up in the pile of books I want to read some day. I was nervous the person who gave it to me was going to ask if I'd read it, so one day at work, I flipped through it. I wanted to at least be able to say, "I've looked at it." Don't judge me. I didn't go into reading it with much excitement. In fact, I was doing the bare minimum. I'm a work in progress. Stop judging me.

What I read in that book radically challenged me. I saw a chapter on communication and decided to start there. It wasn't the first chapter of the book, but it looked interesting to me. That chapter rocked my world, little country girl. I had never in my life read how communication was about understanding and not agreeing. From there I moved to the first chapter of the book. On my flight to Israel I reread the chapter on communication. I had read it once before, but this time it was in order of the other chapters. When I finished that chapter, I instantly felt the conviction from the Holy Spirit. I thought about that former staff member. Up until that point I didn't see how I was wrong in my response. Because I believed this person's thinking and attitude was toxic, I felt justified in my response. That's what jerks do. Jerks justify behaviors at the expense of others. On the plane reading that chapter, I instantly knew just how wrong I was. When I got home, I apologized for my response.

Up until that moment I felt justified whenever I became passionate because it only came out when others were disrespectful and wrong. There was a part of me that felt they deserved what they got. That type of thinking communicated that I was the only person who mattered in the relationship. If I could do it over again, I would seek to understand first. I would have asked more questions. I would have communicated, "I understand you are frustrated. I want to help, but I can't have you telling the boss you won't do something. Help me understand why this frustrated you so much." Then after I had listened, if I still didn't agree, I would have said, "I hear that you are frustrated. Let me share another perspective."

When we seek to understand, we show we care. We also show that the other person matters. When we seek to understand, the other person's defenses go down. When we seek to understand, we show that the other person matters. Then, after understanding, we can share a different perspective.

A Different Perspective

Having a different perspective is not wrong. We just have to understand that a different perspective also doesn't mean that others are wrong. When someone else is truly wrong in their thinking, we can offer a different perspective only after we have sought to understand where they are coming from. We may still not agree, but will do so cordially and save the relationship with both people feel understood.

A great way to do this is to repeat back what someone has said, but in your own words. Before you offer a different perspective, repeat what you've heard and then give a chance for them to respond. For example, "What I hear you saying is *Die Hard* is not a Christmas movie because you do not like violence and action at Christmas. It doesn't feel warm and magical like other Christmas classics. Is that what you are saying?" If it is, and you still disagree, then you can reply, "Can I share a different perspective?" I understand that *Die Hard* is not a traditional Christmas movie. I get that it's not warm and magical for some. To me it's a Christmas movie because not everyone's Christmas is warm and magical feeling. If your Christmas party was, God forbid, attacked by terrorists, would it no longer be a Christmas party? Does the bad act of the terrorists stop the fact that there are Christmas decorations, songs, and references? "Now I have a machine gun, ho, ho, ho" may not be everyone's cup of tea, but it is undeniably Christmas. Then at this point they will reply,

"You are right. It's not my type of Christmas movie, but I now know that it is in fact a Christmas movie." Yippee ki-yay!

If only if it were that easy. People may not instantly agree with you when you show you care for them, but you have a greater chance of being heard when you first show that you are trying to hear the other person. The example is silly, but I've tried it in real life and it worked. Multiple times in fact.

Here's what doesn't work: arguing, name-calling, yelling, attacking. People can change their opinions, but they don't when they are feeling attacked. The very fact that disagreements feel like attacks on our identity means we have to be intentional to not allow the gap of disagreement to impact our relationship. We think that if we yell, argue, fuss, nag, or put down, we can wear someone down. Does it work? I know it's the natural response, but does it work? The definition of insanity is doing the same things over and over again and expecting different results. If fighting, arguing, giving the silent treatment, yelling, etc. is helping you have healthy relationships, then keep going. It's working. I personally have yet to find a person who has healthy relationships and unhealthy communication practices. You can be right and still be in the wrong by how you communicate.

Even when you seek to understand there are some things that you will never agree on. In those moments you may have to agree to simply not talk about that subject. For the health of the relationship it's not worth bringing up ______ topic.

If you are not being physically harmed, emotionally harmed, and or the argument isn't mission critical, then agree to disagree. Respect one another's difference, and don't bring it up. The relationship is too important to do so. There are way more things that we agree on than disagree on. Find those and talk about them. This is how we can disagree and still be friends. Once we get this down, we can move to the third part of James message. Anger! Dun, dun, dun!

You Won't Like Me When I'm Angry

Now, when we are quick to listen and slow to speak, then we will be slow to become angry. These first two are so crucial. Then James says, we should be slow to anger. I covered anger pretty extensively so far in this book. It's so important because often our anger causes others to feel unsafe and causes us to regret our actions.

I love the following quote:

> Speak when you are angry and you'll make the best speech you'll ever regret. (Laurence J. Peter)

This is why it's so important to take a little time to process your strong emotions. We are not the best version of ourselves when we are angry. When a rattlesnake is cornered, sometimes it becomes so angry that it bites itself. When a person harbors anger or bitterness in their heart, they are poisoning themselves just like the rattlesnake that bites itself. This is why I believe we need some time to process our emotions. By the way, I have never seen a rattlesnake do this. I read about it online, and as we all know, if it's on the Internet, it must be true. Don't miss the point though. The point is often in our anger we do damage to ourselves.

Stuffers and Spillers

Remember the section on stuffers and spillers from chapter 5? Stuffers bury the emotion deep down hoping to never have to deal with it. Spillers explode with emotions and just want to express it.

When a stuffer is unchecked, they will bury the emotions deep. What is buried eventually has a way of exploding out, and when it does it will not be pretty. On the other hand, spillers often vent until they feel better no matter the cost.

The twenty-four-hour rule is crucial for spillers and stuffers. For spillers it gives time to calm down and make sure you stay respectful. For stuffers it's important because it ensures that you communicate frustration before the expiration date. For the most part, when you hold on to frustration the other person moves on. When you finally spill out, they struggle to remember what the issue even is. Anger is such a strong emotion; we need to handle it with care.

Let's Wrap This Up

James gives amazing wisdom for why anger is a killer in relationships:

> Because human anger does not produce the righteousness that God desires. (James 1:20)

Human anger does not produce the righteousness that God desires. Human anger may produce quick results, but in the long run, it doesn't change hearts or minds. Anger may lead others to fear us. Anger may lead others to tiptoe around us. Anger may lead us to feel in control, but at the end of the day, it doesn't get long-term results. That's why the goal of communication is so important.

The goal of communication is understanding, not agreement.

I want to have relationships with people I disagree with. Otherwise, I'm building a kingdom where everyone looks like, thinks like, and talks like me. That's egotistical. I can communicate what I disagree with after I show I understand. This takes lots of practice. It's not natural to seek to understand first, but we don't serve a natural God. We serve a supernatural God who has given us everything we need to have healthy relationships by killing the jerk. For Christians this is a serious challenge. Remember, James wrote this to Christians. For non-Christians their anger represents themselves, their politics, or maybe their family. For Christians our anger represents God. Human anger does not produce the righteousness that God desires. We think our anger will change someone, but it doesn't. Empathy and understanding have a chance to change someone. Anger creates a divide. We are human, so there are times when we lose our cool, but we need to be working on representing Jesus well in all areas of our life. This includes how we communicate with others.

This chapter's Win: Write down the goal of communication and put it somewhere you can see it often. The goal of communication is understanding, not agreeing. When you feel yourself disagreeing, look to the goal of communication.

Questions for Further Reflection

1. When it comes to communication, how would you rate yourself? On a scale of 1 to 10 (1 being amazing at communication and 10 being horrible), where would you rate yourself and why?
2. Why didn't you pick a lower number?
3. Why would it be important for you to change how you communicate with others?
4. What would it take for you to move up and become a better communicator?
5. What would your relationships look like if you understood before you spoke?

CHAPTER 9

Practice Not Being a Jerk

All relationships have issues. There are no perfect friendships, jobs, marriages, or families. Every person you will ever meet is flawed, and because of that relationships will be challenging. Two broken people do not make one whole person. It always feels great in the movies when we hear a star-crossed love interest say, "You complete me," but it's unrealistic. When you look for someone to complete, you are waiting to be let down. Imagine taking a glass and breaking it, then taking a separate glass and breaking it. If you picked up the pieces of both glasses that remained intact and tried to put them together, they would not fit each other. It's the same with us as humans. We are all broken in different ways. Trying to become completed by a broken human just doesn't work. Instead we need become whole by becoming a new creation.

> Therefore, if anyone is in Christ, the new creation has come: The old has gone, the new is here! (2 Cor. 5:17)

We are born broken, but through Jesus we become new creations. I love psychology and learning, but I've yet to read anything that helps explain why we are so broken as humans. On our own we find ways to self-destruct. Looking for another broken person to make you happy is a recipe for disaster. Until you are happy within, another broken person cannot complete you. It's like what the great theologian Lauren Hill once sang, "How you gonna win when, you ain't right within?" Through Jesus we become new creations. The old way of thinking is gone. Instead of looking to another broken human to fix us, we find healing in Jesus.

We sin so often we don't even keep track of them. We may remember the big ones, but it's easy to forget the little ones. At the same time, we want others to show us grace for our sin while we seek vengeance for others that sin against us. We are a broken people. The times I chose to do what I wanted even though it negatively impacted others was sin. The times I didn't do what I should have done was sin. We don't like to think about our sin. It's sad and can be shameful. Unless we look at our sin through the lens of God's love. God didn't send Jesus to die for perfect people. He sent him to die for sinners in which I am the worst. It's not a competition, but I can sin with the best of them. Thank God for grace. God loves me not because I've been occasionally good, but despite the fact that I've royally messed up. I love the lyrics from the old hymn "It Is Well with My Soul."

> My sin, oh, the bliss of this glorious thought
> My sin, not in part but the whole,
> Is nailed to the cross, and I bear it no more,
> Praise the Lord, praise the Lord, o my soul

It's impossible to know the love of God if you don't self-reflect on your sin. I don't dwell on my sin, but I'm aware of my sin. We don't like to think of our bad choices. We don't like to think of our selfishness, but we won't run to God if we don't understand just how jacked up we are. This isn't to shame us. Shame has no place in your life. More on this in chapter 11. You have worth because you are God's creation, but you also have some selfishness inside you. Until we wrestle with this, we cannot know the love of God. It's difficult to treat others the way you want to be treated when you haven't come to terms with just how much sin God has forgiven in you. It is by grace we are transformed. That is, it is when we realize how jacked up we are, then we can start to fathom how loving God is. When we receive the grace of God, it renews us to become new creations.

That's why I believe this book is so important. Kill the jerk and become the person God has wired you to be. Allow Jesus to complete you, become whole, and then you'll be able to treat others how you want to be treated. Until then, we will keep lashing back at others because they haven't "completed us." Not only that but until we become healthy and whole emotionally, we will find ways to self-destruct our relationships. When we are not whole, we look for quick fixes for our brokenness. We end up self destructing with food, pornography, alcohol, or other extreme forms of quick fixes.

We know no one is perfect, and yet many people believe we have to pretend to be perfect in order to be accepted. We do not like exposing our flaws and issues. This fear of rejection is often a major issue in relationships. When we work harder on pretending to perfect than on our issues, there is a problem. We often think we are better than we are because we are so good at acting we believe our own performance. It's exhausting to pretend to be better than we really are. It's also exhausting to not get anywhere. Progress is energizing! Writing of progress, let's progress to the next paragraph.

It Takes Practice

You can have healthy relationships, but it takes practice. Sometimes it seems impossible to have healthy relationships. Relationships are difficult, messy, frustrating, and unpredictable. Way too many people settle into a mediocre or even toxic relationship because they just don't think healthy relationships are possible. Or maybe the work seems so daunting they simply freeze and then accept the status quo. Here is the key: healthy relationships happen intentionally, not accidentally. If you want to have great relationships, you cannot simply hope for it. It is not always convenient. It's not always easy. But it's so worth it! Healthy relationships are possible with some practice.

Most people hope to have great relationships but aren't willing to do the work to have them. Hope is an amazing feeling but a terrible strategy. You can have healthy relationships, but it takes work. Anything worth having takes work. I can't hope to have a six pack of abs while I eat pizza and binge watch the TV show *The Office* for the twelfth time. I know, I've tried. I know all things are possible with the Lord, but He has yet to bless me with abs of steel on a pizza diet. You truly can have healthy relationships, but it is going to take some hard work on yourself. We often wish or demand others to change, but we cannot control other people. We cannot force anyone to change. We often work harder at thinking about other people's issues than we do working on our own. Part of killing the jerk is working on becoming less of one. I know it may be scary, but it's worth pushing through the fear. Set up the appointment to see a counselor, develop a plan to work on your issues, make a regularly scheduled hangout with someone you love. Seek forgiveness in Jesus and have him replace your brokenness with a new heart. I don't know what your next step is, but I do know when it's intentional it's impactful.

Reading this book and others that focus on healthy relationships are a great intentional step to learn. You can have healthy relationships, but it doesn't start with anyone else but you. You cannot control other people, you cannot force other people to change, and you cannot improve yourself as long as you think everyone else is the jerk. The truth is that when you are healthy, other people will be forced to either become healthy themselves or they will leave.

Take gossip for example. Typically, the people that are involved with gossip say something along the lines of, "I don't mean to gossip. So many people come to me because I'm a safe person." That may be true, but if they are bad-mouthing others, they are coming to you because you allow it. You cannot control other people coming to you, but you can control how you respond. For the gossip a response of, "I'm sorry you are going through that. You need to talk to the person you are upset with. If I can help you do that, I will. If not, then I cannot help you with this." If you say that statement, it won't take long for the gossipers to change or stop coming to you. The real issue is we often like our toxic or harmful behaviors. The gossip may say so many people come to them, but more than likely a gossip loves the excitement of hearing dirt on others. The same is true with almost any unhealthy behavior. Unhealthy things grow naturally and most of the time in the dark. Expose them to the light, and they will either leave or they will have a clear understanding of what they need to do to change.

It's natural to be unhealthy. As humans we do not naturally drift to excellence. I wish we did. If we did we wouldn't need as much government, bosses, parental guidance, teachers, budgets, coaches, or diets. Healthy relationships come intentionally, not accidentally. It takes intentional effort and lots of practice.

Whether it's having a short fuse and losing your temper, believing the worst about people you love, feeling out of control when you're are not in control, being passive-aggressive, or any other unhealthy response, your reactions should not be dictated by others' behaviors. Instead, our reactions should reflect Jesus. There are no magic pills to make this happen. There are no easy buttons. If you want to be great at relationships, then it's going to take good old-fashion practice.

Yes, Allen Iverson, We Are Talking about Practice

I don't like the idea of practice. I like the idea of naturally being great at things. What I've learned is what is natural to me is often unhealthy, broken, and selfish. I am a naturally good overeater. I could win an Olympic gold medal in overeating. That's natural to me. What's unnatural is disciplining myself to a diet. There are lots of things that we do naturally well, and many of them are destructive to who we ultimately want to be. What's unnatural takes something supernatural to change. The Scripture says,

> Finally, brothers and sisters, whatever is true, whatever is noble, whatever is right, whatever is pure, whatever is lovely, whatever is admirable—if anything is excellent or praiseworthy—think about

> such things. Whatever you have learned or received or heard from me, or seen in me—put it into *practice*. And the God of peace will be with you. (Phil. 4:8–9)

Did you catch what the verses said? Our words flow out of our thoughts; therefore, we have to work on thinking about whatever is true, noble, right, pure, lovely, admirable, excellent, and praiseworthy. How do we do that? The truth is, most of those thoughts listed in the Scripture are not natural. Especially when I don't get my way. We all have a jerk inside of us, and we also can intentionally do something about him. The answer is found at the end of the verse. You put it into practice.

> Practice! We talkin' bout practice? (Allen Iverson)[6]

Why am I talking about former NBA superstar Allen Iverson? If you don't know, Google "Allen Iverson Practice." You are welcome.

Practice. Practice is what separates the greats from everyone else. In Malcolm Gladwell's book *Outlier*, he points out: It takes ten thousand hours to become an expert at anything! It doesn't matter whether it's athletics, academics, or relationships. According to Gladwell, there are no "naturals." You have to put in the time. Generally speaking, the only difference between an elite person in any field and everybody else is a few thousand hours of practice time.[7]

---

[6] Allen Iverson, NBA press conference, May 8, 2002.

[7] Malcolm Gladwell, *Outlier*, 2008.

I know talking about practice isn't glamorous, but practice is what prepares us for greatness. The issue in most relationships is we've spent ten thousand hours practicing the wrong things. Because it's natural to be selfish, angry, insecure, etc., we have unintentionally practiced the wrong behaviors so much we have become great at not being great at relationships. Way too many Christians are under the guise that walking with Jesus is natural. It's like, if I say a little prayer, then I'll be transformed. That's a nice thought, but rarely how God works. Salvation is a free gift from God, but Scripture says we are to work out our salvation. God has given us everything we need to live a godly life, but it doesn't come by being passive. It comes with practice.

Some of your worst behaviors can be solved with practicing the right things. We have unintentionally spent our lives practicing the wrong behaviors. We are so accustomed to simply flying off the handle, shutting down, using manipulation, fighting unfair, trying to control others, etc. that we feel it is just who we are. If who you are hurts others, then it's time to change. We all have personality quirks, annoying habits, and differences in relating styles. If saying, "That's just who I am," is a rationalization for ungodly behavior, then know that's the inner jerk talking and not Jesus. You are better than that. I know you are. I know because God didn't make junk. We are all broken and in process, but the God of the universe has given us everything we need to snuff out the inner jerk. Making excuses for the jerk is not helpful.

What if instead of letting the jerk control you, you intentionally work on controlling the jerk?

When it comes to following Jesus, it takes some practice. If the 10K hour rule to become an expert is right, then I think it also applies to following Jesus. No one is great at it overnight. We like to think that as soon as we become a

Christian our issues go away. That's simply not true. Every person who has ever followed Jesus struggled.

Show me someone who can pray in public, and I'll show you someone who has spent some time practicing praying in private. Show me someone who has bold faith in public, and I'll show you someone who has practiced taking 10K plus steps of faith in their lifetime. Show me someone who is kind to the least of these, and I'll show you someone who has practiced being kind to their family and friends. Think about it just for a second. Have you ever noticed how it's easier to be kind to strangers than to our own family members? We have to work hard and not letting the jerk out. This is why if you have little kids or have had little kids, they are often way better to their teachers or the babysitter than they are for you. Jerks. They are their true selves around their parents because they feel safe. That means that as parents we see their extra silly side that they won't show others. It means we see their best and their worst. We see their true selves, and that means we see their jerk side. Adults aren't much better.

I'm convinced that one of the reasons we are all so tired as adults is because we have to work so hard to not let our true selves come out while we are at work or around our friends. It's exhausting keeping the jerk at bay all day. At the same time, it's also exhausting being a jerk. It's exhausting being angry and offended all the time. That's why we cannot simply ignore the jerk. We must intentionally make the jerk subject to Jesus.

Whatever!

When it comes to relationships, we often want uphill results with downhill effort. The way to become better, more kind, and more loving is to put your faith into practice. Paul addressed this in his amazing letter to the church in Philippi. Let's break down what Paul wrote:

> Finally, brothers and sisters, whatever is true, whatever is noble, whatever is right, whatever is pure, whatever is lovely, whatever is admirable—if anything is excellent or praiseworthy—think about such things. (Phil. 4:8)

For those that are less than optimistic this would be a great thing to permanently put somewhere you can see it often. Print it, have it put on a painting, tattoo it on your body. You get the point. This is such a great verse. When negative thoughts come to your mind, Paul says to say, "Whatever!" Whatever is true, noble, right, pure, lovely, admirable, if anything is excellent or praiseworthy—think about it. Now, who controls the thoughts that go through your head? I don't know. I don't know where some of my crazy thoughts come from. Satan, hormones, lies I have believed, and that late-night Taco Bell run are all suspects to the creators of my crazy thoughts. Not every thought that goes through our head is a thought worthy of having. When the jerk comes, you have to retire his thinking and that takes practice. The jerk doesn't go away naturally or quietly. When a thought comes that is not true, noble, right, pure, lovely, admirable, excellent or praiseworthy, I have a choice to make. I can let that thought take over, or I can choose to make it subject to Jesus.

During one season of my life where I felt wronged by someone else, I was allowing negative thoughts dominate my mind. I would feel okay as long as I was around other people, but any time I was alone, my brain went to my pain, hurt, and disappointment. It was unhealthy. One day I was driving, and the negative thoughts were consuming me. I started saying this verse out loud. It didn't help. The thoughts were too big. Too painful. So I said the verse out loud again, but this time it was even louder. Still nothing. I ended up yelling at the top of my lungs, "*Whatever is true, noble, right, pure, lovely, admirable, excellent, or praiseworthy—think about such things*!" I'm sure I looked ridiculous to the other drivers. I was at a stop light, and I yelled so loud I know the other drivers could hear me. You want to know what happened next? It worked. The negative thoughts died down. I laughed at how ridiculous I looked, and a smile came to my face. It was natural to think about the worst. It takes intentional practice of the right things to change.

In fact, the undisciplined mind thinks about the worst of things. A disciplined mind chooses to think about what is best.

According to Dr. Rick Hanson, "Negative stimuli produce more neural activity than do equally intense (e.g., loud, bright) positive ones. They are also perceived more easily and quickly. The alarm bell of your brain—the amygdala[8] (you've got two of these little nuggets, one on either side of your head)—uses about two-thirds of its neurons to look for bad news: it's primed to go negative."

Once it sounds the alarm, negative events and experiences get quickly stored in your memory. It takes no effort to retain a negative experience. In contrast to a positive experience, it takes an intentional effort to think about a positive thought for twelve seconds or more in order for that positive thought to move from short-term memory to long term.

---

[8] Dr. Rick Hansen, https://www.rickhanson.net/how-your-brain-makes-you-easily-intimidated/

To put it simply, the brain is like super glue for negative thoughts and oil and water for positive thoughts. This is why one bad thing makes you feel as if you've had a horrible day. You would think that if more good than bad happened we would have a good day. Often the entire analysis of our day is based on one negative event. Every day when I get home from work, I ask my kids to put a number to their day between 1 and 10. One being awful and ten being awesome. Whenever one of them has a low number, I ask why. Here is a typical response: "My day is a 3 because JoJo (not the kid's real name) bumped me on the playground." I follow this up by asking what else happened. The typical response I hear is, "Nothing! That's it!" So everything else went great at school, but because of one accident, the whole day went down the toilet? "Yes." That same type of thing happens to us adults as well. One negative event is heavier than the positive ones.

Our brains are somewhat broken in that we focus on the negative. You add to that the amount of negative news out there, and it's no wonder humans are so negative all the time. Listen, some of your brains can't handle all the bad news you are exposing it to. Some of you need to cut out the 24-hour news channels. Some of you need to cut out some of your entertainment. Some people need to get off social media. If there is something that is making you feel less than, angry, or down and you can separate yourself from it, you should! It is literally leading your brain to freak out. If you are mad a lot, check what you are feeding your brain. If you are unhappy, check your thoughts. If your brain is holding on to the negative, choose to practice thinking about things that are true, noble, pure, etc. There are some bad things that we cannot filter, and this is where practice comes in. We are all naturally jerks in one way or another. To kill the jerk, it takes intentional practice.

The next time you start to go negative intentionally start thinking about twelve things you are grateful for. Being grateful and thinking about the right things actually rewires your brain. "UCLA's Mindful Awareness Research Center found that regularly expressing gratitude changes the molecular structure of your brain, keeps your gray matter functioning, and makes you healthier and happier."[9] I love when science backs up what Scripture teaches!

So what did Paul say? He gave us seven things to think about.

Think about it:
Whatever is true.
Whatever is noble.
Whatever is right.
Whatever is pure.
Whatever admirable.
Whatever is excellent.
Whatever is praiseworthy.

The jerk is the opposite of everything on this list. The jerk focuses on what's not true, what is wrong, what is impure, what is disrespectful, what is sloppy or lazy, and what is negative. To kill the jerk, we have to intentionally focus on things that are the opposite of the jerk.

I'm going to be vulnerable with you guys. I trust you'll not hold this against me. Loyalty is really important to me. If I consider you a friend, then you are a friend for life. I've never in my life broken up with a friend. I don't hide people on Facebook, and I don't unfriend people on social media. I try to practice the idea that we can be friends and disagree. I

[9] https://jimkwik.com/kwik-brain-047/

try to be loyal and faithful to my friends. At the exact same time I'm overly worried my friends will leave me. When it comes to people who I am friends with, I have some negativity bias. I have some wounds that have led me to have some insecurity when it comes to friendship.

When I was in the tenth grade one of my best friends let me know that he had a new circle of friends and that meant he had too many friends to be close with. He quoted to me the Bible verse, "A man of too many friends comes to ruin, but there is a friend who sticks closer than a brother" (Prov. 18:24). He left off the last part of the verse. Oh, and he took that verse completely out of context. The point of that verse is a crowd doesn't make great friends. There are lots of people who will want to be around you during the good times, but there are only a few people who will stick closer than a brother. When the poo hits the fan, most people leave (jerks!) but there are some people who will stick by your side no matter what. Those are good friends.

When he said that to me, it wrecked me. Often the negative events that shape our lives tend to come from experiences that confirm our insecurities. I was not a confident kid. When my friend said this to me, it impacted me because it confirmed what I already believed about myself: I'm not good enough. Thankfully, by the grace of God, I've been able to experience God's love in such a way that my insecurity is less. I've become secure in knowing that I am who God says I am. At that moment though, I was wrecked.

Since then I have had to battle my thoughts when it comes to friends. There is this insecurity that says if I drop the ball or let them down, then the friendship will be over. I am convinced that if someone sees my inner jerk they will leave me. I've locked on to a negative emotion. I let one negative experience define how I feel about friends. But Paul says you've got to think about whatever is true. I have had friends leave, but I've had way more friends stick by my side. To this day, very often when I see an e-mail, text, or Facebook message that says, "Can we talk," my natural thought is to assume the worst. I immediately jump to how I was not good enough and now someone else I love is going to leave. That is, my brains go to position. I've had to intentionally talk myself off many proverbial ledges. Practice really does make a difference. When I get a call and my natural thought is someone is going to leave, I intentionally replace that thought with truth. They may leave, but that doesn't mean I'm not good enough. I cannot control them; I can only love others the way God has loved me. From there I convince myself that they are not going to leave because we are truly friends. I'm not perfect at this, but I'm so much better than when this wound first happened.

Enough about me, let's talk about you.

The temptation is to allow your day to be defined by the negative experience you have. You've got to take that thought captive and make it obedient to Jesus. In other words, you have to practice becoming an optimist. Some people seem to be negative about everything. Some people are negative about everything except their negativity. When you ask a negative person about their negativity, they often become optimistic and say, "I'm not being negative! I'm a realist." You might be a realist in your own mind, but to others you may be a person who is being optimistic about their own negativity.

Negativity breeds negativity. It's like a cancer. You have to choose what you are going to allow your brain to think about. So if your boss has some flaws that you see, you better choose to focus on his or her strengths or you are going to become miserable at your job. If your spouse has some negative flaws, you cannot ignore them but you better choose to think about the positive things they do. If your friend annoys you because they are always late, you have to choose to think about the great things your friend brings to the table. This doesn't mean we ignore harmful behaviors. It simply means we protect ourselves from magnifying a misdemeanor and thus turning it into a felony. Please note this: truly harmful behaviors should not be overlooked. Leave a boss that's abusive, find a counselor if your relationship is toxic, or separate if you have some unhealthy friends that are pulling you down. This is not what I'm writing about. Way too often we turn good people into Hitler because we don't get our way, they do it differently than we do, or because we're control freaks. Way too often we let a misdemeanor destroy an otherwise great day. On those days we need to rewire our brains.

People will always let you down to some degree. In the same way you will always let someone else down. Whether your inner jerk is a monster or a little pest, he has to be addressed intentionally. What will it take for you to no longer allow the jerk inside to control the way you respond to other people? You've got to practice turning negative into positives. Look how Paul ends this section. This is so good.

> Whatever you have learned or received or heard from me, or seen in me—put it into *practice*. And the God of peace will be with you. (Phil. 4:9)

Practice. We talkin' 'bout practice. Not a game. Not a game. Practice. Yes, Allen Iverson,[10] we are talking about

---

[10] NBA Hall of Farmer, Allen Iverson has a famous rant where he says the word *practice* a million times. It's legendary.

practice. Whatever you have seen in the life of Paul, put it into practice.

Now this wouldn't mean much if it was written by a millionaire preacher who had never struggled a day in his life. That's not the case with Paul. Paul wrote this while being chained to a Roman guard in prison. He was in prison because he felt God was telling him to tell others about Jesus. He didn't commit a crime. In fact, at one point the only reason they kept Paul in prison is because the guy who was in charge wanted to hear more about this Jesus guy Paul kept preaching about. Jerk. Just for a second imagine how you would handle Paul's situation? We cannot control other people or every situation we are in. To try and control it will make us miserable. Asking "Why?" will lead us nowhere good. Our only hope is to rely on the strength of Jesus to work on controlling ourselves.

So Paul found a way to be joyful despite difficult circumstances—practice that. Paul says the God of peace will be with you when you practice the right thinking. If you can't find joy in the midst of your day, it's most likely because you are focused on one negative aspect and not choosing to focus on what is true. This isn't easy, but it's possible. With practice you can see the world through a better lens.

For years I said I don't run. I hated running. In fact, my exact line was, "If you see me running, please help me because someone or something is chasing me." There were few things in life I hated less than running: Nazis, roaches, slow Wi-Fi, the devil, the Boston Celtics, Indiana Jones and Kingdom of the Crystal Skull, and then running. I literally own a shirt that says, and I quote, "I wanted to go jogging but Proverbs 28:1 says, 'The wicked run when no one is chasing them,' so there's that."

Back then I was working out at the YMCA, and because I decided to quit my job and plant a church, we no longer could afford to pay for the gym membership. I needed a way to exercise, and so I decided to sign up for a 5K and run. I didn't want to, but paying for a race made me accountable to exercise daily. It was straight awful! Not only was it awful but I paid money for something I can do for free. I couldn't figure out what is wrong with the people who say they enjoy this activity. The first time I went out to run I couldn't run a mile. I ran half a mile, and it felt like I drank a big glass of death. But I set a goal, so I went out and endured some more pain. It stunk! Eventually, running half a mile wasn't as difficult. Then a mile became easy. I kept going until I was ready for the 5K. On the day of my 5K, I remember two things. I remember I got up really early and ate a bowl of Frosted Flakes. Why? Because they're great! Well, that was a bad decision because I got a cramp a half mile into the race. It hurt so bad. The other thing I remember is I ran the race with my brother and he was just a little faster than me. He stepped in dog poo, and I could smell it the entire race because I was just behind him. A year before running that race a cramp would have been enough for me to give up running forever. Throw in the smell of dog poo, and you have me vowing to end running around the world. I'd throw a march where we would walk against running. I'd raise money to elect government officials who would ban running. I would no longer say I had a runny nose. It would be drippy but not runny. I had a low tolerance to running pain but on that day I finished the race. Why? Practice. Not only that but I went on to run a 10k. I then became full of stupid and I signed up for a half marathon. I ran the entire half marathon in the pouring rain. I had trained so well I didn't mind the rain. I wore a T-shirt that said, "Running Sucks!" and finished my first half marathon with a smile on my face. It was awesome! I endured a lot of blisters, bloody toes, cramps, and pain to get to a place where I could run a half marathon. From there I went to run a total of three half marathons. Since then I've run multiple races. I'm never the fastest, but my rule of thumb is if you are not last you are first. As long as I am not the last to finish, I feel good about finishing the race. They always tell the results based on age. Jerks. I wish they would do it based on weight. I know I would be one of the fastest in my weight class. I'm also one of the only people in my weight class that runs. Today, I am no longer afraid of running. I still don't like it, but I know I can do it because I've put in the pain, I mean, practice.

Today people are freaking out about all sorts of things. Our freak-out levels are incredibly high. What does Paul say? Put the right things into practice. It may be difficult, but with some practice it becomes easier. But you've got to practice. Practice thinking about what it true, noble, lovely, admirable, excellent or praiseworthy. Practice thinking about things that are life giving instead of life taking. Life change is difficult, but so is anything worth having. Being a jerk is natural. Being kind takes intentionality and great strength.

Many people are comfortable with their jerk. It's all they've known. But you won't grow until you stretch yourself. You stretch yourself by practicing something you are not naturally good at.

The truth is the jerk is difficult to kill because we make excuses for him. He's been a part of our life for so long we think, *This is just the way I am.* That's true. That's why practice is so crucial.

The jerk doesn't leave quietly or quickly. It takes time, effort, and intentional practice to become good at relationships. You'll fail often, but just make sure you are failing forward. Every time we fail, we have an opportunity to learn and grow. If we choose to grow from the experience and continue to practice, we can see great amounts of change. Life change is rarely an instant moment. It's more often a collection of consistent decisions in the right direction.

When it comes to relationships, people are anxious to improve their circumstances but are unwilling to improve themselves; therefore, they remain broken. When we understand that we cannot control other people but we can work on controlling ourselves, then we are at the beginning of life change. Until we do the hard work of looking inward and allowing Jesus to work on our hearts, we will be stuck in a cycle of blaming others for our unhappy circumstances.

Are you ready to commit to work on your inner jerk? You cannot control other people. You cannot control what others do or say. You can only practice controlling yourself. Here's the truth of the matter: greatness comes from what you do consistently, not occasionally. So if you want to kill the jerk it will be a lifelong commitment. It's so worth it. Healthy relationships are worth the difficult work it takes to have them. It just takes practice.

The Win: Set aside time to practice what you learned in this chapter. Once a day intentionally practice being grateful. Thank God for the positive things you have in your life. It should not take you more than a few minutes. These minutes could have an amazing impact on the rest of your day.

Questions for Further Reflection

1. Out of the list Paul gives us in Philippians 4:8, which one do you struggle to think about the most?
2. What is the opposite of whichever item you picked from that verse?
3. How can you intentionally think about the one characteristic you picked from Philippians 4:8?
4. What would it look like if you were more like this one characteristic?
5. How can you practice this behavior intentionally this week?

CHAPTER 10

Pride Is the Jerk's Best Friend

The jerk thrives on pride. Since we all have an inner jerk, every one of us has some issue with pride. Pride focuses on the issues of others, refuses to say sorry, overestimates one's worth, and exaggerates one's faults. Pride impacts relationships but has an even bigger effect on individuals. The psalmist in Scripture wrote,

> In his pride the wicked man does not seek him; in all his thoughts there is no room for God. (Ps. 10:4)

According to the psalmist, pride is the reason a person does not seek God. Specifically, a prideful person has no room for God in their life. Jerk. Now, in order to get the most out of this Scripture, we have to understand what pride is. Not all pride is wrong. In fact, healthy and emotionally whole people know how to feel the healthy version of pride. For example, I'm proud of my wife and the hard work she puts into her job. I'm proud of my kids when they do well in school. I'm proud of the church I lead. When you work hard and do what you say you'll do, it produces a healthy pride.

Psychologists distinguish between two kinds of pride.

1. Authentic pride—Authentic pride arises when we feel good about ourselves, confident, and productive, and is related to socially-desirable personality traits such as being agreeable, conscientious, and emotionally stable.

   Authentic pride is something that you should feel. In fact, someone who struggles with being prideful has a hard time feeling authentic pride. Let me show you why.
2. Hubristic pride—Hubristic pride tends to involve egotism and arrogance and is related to socially undesirable traits such as being disagreeable, aggressive, having low or brittle self-esteem, and being prone to shame.

   Hubristic pride is the type of pride that rubs us the wrong way. The interesting thing is when we struggle with pride, it's often a result of low self-esteem or being prone to shame (See the next chapter).

This is what makes pride such a tricky monster. Often the people who struggle with pride are blind to it because they don't see it for what it really is. Pride and insecurity go together. Show me someone who has a low view of themselves, and I'll show you someone who has some major pride issues. Pride can mean a lot of things, but for this chapter we are going to define it as this:

Pride—an inflated view of oneself.

Pride is all about you. And either you think too highly of yourself or you think too lowly of yourself. Either way both are a result of pride. Pride is jerk!

The Two-Headed Monster of Pride

Pride is fueled by two things that seem to contradict one another. Because pride is an inflated view of oneself, it finds its fuel in two extremes.

The Two-Headed Monster of Pride:

1. Success
2. Failure

Pride is an inflated view of oneself, so when pride finds success it becomes a monster and when pride finds failure it becomes a monster. Think about how this can impact you spiritually. Let's look at our verse again:

> In his pride the wicked man does not seek him; in all his thoughts there is no room for God. (Ps. 10:4)

This is not talking about the good form of pride. This is the negative form. And pride causes us to not seek God. So when life is good, pride leads us to say I don't need God. When we make mistakes, pride leads us to say my sin is too big for God. Tim Keller writes, "Pride is the carbon monoxide of sin. It silently and slowly kills you without you even knowing it."

You see when you make yourself the center of the universe everything you do is a lot bigger deal than it really is. When you succeed, it's the best thing ever, and when you fail, it's the worst thing ever. Pride says, "I'm the best" and "I'm the worse." It's why some can't get over sin. It's pride. Pride makes us hide sin because we are afraid that someone will find out that we are imperfect. Pride also makes us feel our sin is too big for God to forgive. Jesus looked out at the men who were crucifying Him and said, "Father, forgive them for they don't know what they are doing." Jesus forgave the men who physically beat and killed him on a bloody cross, and yet you think He can't forgive your sin? That's *pride*! God has seen it all. We can't do anything to impress God, and we can't do anything to depress God.

So our Scripture says the prideful have no room for God, and that's also our Big Idea for this chapter.

Big Idea: The prideful have no room for God.

Is there a chance your pride is getting in the way of what God wants to do in your life? Is your pride causing you to hide your sin? Is your pride causing you to avoid God? Do not wait until you have a crisis moment in life. It's an amazing thing walking with God through all seasons. Way too many people wait until their world falls apart to come to God. During a great season of life, it's easy to feel we don't need God. Just imagine how much better that season would be if we included God? Many people can relate to coming to God because their world fell apart. The truth is, way too many people cannot handle success because of pride.

Success Is a Faith Slayer

Often the greatest enemy of our faith is success.

When life is good it's easy for pride to creep in and say you don't need God. It is difficult to be a Christian in America. It's difficult because of the amazing freedom and blessings we have. Christianity thrives during times of persecution. In America it's easy to be a cushy Christian. As long as my bills are paid, my health is okay, and my Lakers are winning, I'm good with God. I'm not above praying for God to intervene on behalf of my Lakers. I love the famous quote by C. S. Lewis:

> It would seem that Our Lord finds our desires not too strong, but too weak. We are half-hearted creatures, fooling about with drink and sex and ambition when infinite joy is offered us, like an ignorant child who wants to go on making mud pies in a slum because he cannot imagine what is meant by the offer of a holiday at the sea. We are far too easily pleased.

Now, what you need to hear is that there is nothing wrong enjoying life. The quote we just read isn't a slam on living a good life. It's pointing out that we settle for good when infinite joy is offered to us through Jesus. So often we settle because in America we can have good. In Jesus there is so much more. There is so much more than just going to church. There is so much more than just having a religion. In Jesus there is abundant life. Jesus is better than any high, any experience, and any product. Jesus is life, and we so often miss Him because we are satisfied with the good life.

It reminds me of the little girl who had her homework assignment go viral. She wrote 137 words about plain doughnuts. This is glorious.

> You know what I think is weird? Fake donuts, a.k.a. plain ones. I mean, you just stroll into a Dunkin' Doughnuts, and you see all the different flavors and types, like glazed, strawberry, Boston Kreme, and chocolate frosted. And there, just sitting there among all the wonderful flavors, acting like it belongs there, is plain. Right there, laying on the pink and orange tissue paper, with the little shiny silver wall of the crate it's in surrounding it, just like all the real ones. But it's not! It's not one of them! It has no frosting, no sprinkles, no glaze, no cream, no fillings or toppings at all. It shouldn't even be called a doughnut! Or a pastry of any kind! It's just a BAGEL! A BAGEL!

Now, there is nothing wrong with a plain doughnut. I'd still eat them. I don't discriminate against doughnuts. But compared to the greatness that is Boston creme, why would you settle for the plain old doughnut? And that's C. S. Lewis's point. We are far too easily pleased.

One pastor puts it this way:

> Our chief enemy is the lie that says sin will make our future happier. Our chief weapon is the truth that says God will make our future happier. My thirst for joy and meaning and passion are satisfied by the presence and promises of Christ, the power of sin is broken. We do not yield to the offer of sandwich meat when we can smell the steak sizzling on the grill. (Pastor John Piper)

I love that. Pride will wreak havoc on your spiritual life. It will tell you that you are good enough when you succeed and too bad for God's love when you fail. It will lead you to settle for sandwich meat when the steak is sizzling on the grill. Pride will tell you that you are don't need God when you succeed and you're unforgivable when you fail.

The Weapon of Mass Destruction against Pride

In some degree everyone struggles with pride. So how do we fight against pride? One word. Humility.

> When pride comes, then comes disgrace, but with humility comes wisdom. (Prov. 11:2)

Can I be vulnerable with you? I'm in desperate need of God. I love the Enneagram personality profile. If you haven't taken it, then I highly recommend it. What I've learned about myself through this is that my personality comes with insecurity. I am naturally insecure. Like it's in my personality. How messed up is that? So my inflated view of self has to constantly be in check. There are days when I am so hard on myself because of a mistake that it becomes an unhealthy consumption. I often do not feel good enough, qualified enough, or godly enough to lead. The truth is, I'm not. But Jesus through me is. I don't know anything outside of Jesus that helps me have a right view of my life. In Jesus I see that I'm not as bad as my worst mistake and I'm not as great as my greatest success. You see, when I succeed, I know it's in spite of me. On my own I often get in my own way. That's what pride does. Pride says, "Don't ask for help," when what you really need is help. Pride says to hide my flaws when freedom comes from confession. Pride says everyone else is the problem while all along I am the problem. Pride leads me to think that it's all about me. I love the following quote:

> If there's contention in your home, if there's contention in a relationship that you have with your parents or your in-laws or your children or someone in your church or someone in your workplace; always, always, always, the root of that contention is pride. We say, "That other person's sure arrogant." It's not the other person's arrogance. It's my arrogance that causes that contention, having to have my way. (Nancy Leigh DeMoss)[11]

---

[11] https://www.reviveourhearts.com/radio/revive-our-hearts/love-does-not-boast-1/

By nature, I am drawn to think about myself. Jesus is the only thing that helps me take my eyes off myself. But in addition to that Jesus is the only thing that lets me see how I really am. In Jesus I see my pride. In Jesus I know I have success in spite of me, not because of me. In Jesus I know that my failures are covered in His love. Pride causes me to not seek God. That's what our Scripture said. When I fail, pride won't let me seek God because I feel too bad. When I succeed, pride won't let me seek God because I feel I'm too good. Pride is a horrible monster, and the answer is humility.

Four Things That Produce Humility

Humility is difficult to obtain. Many wrongly assume that humility is like the donkey, Eeyore, from *Winnie the Pooh*. Humility is not insecurity. Humility is the choice to put others first. The famous definition of humility from C. S. Lewis says,

> Humility is not thinking less of yourself.
> It's thinking of yourself less.

I'm convinced it is impossible to follow Jesus without humility. Humility is admitting that we don't have all the answers, have limitations, and ultimately need help. Humility is the kryptonite to pride. Where ever there is relational drama, look for the pride. Humility is a belief that other people matter, and so do you. When we get this wrong, we struggle with humility. Humility is not simply believing everyone is better than you. That's insecurity. Humility is understanding that because you are a child of God you have great worth—and so does everyone else. It's not a competition. It's a tension. When we fail to put others first, it is a sign of inflated view of oneself. When we fail to take care of ourselves, it's the other side of the pride coin.

For healthy relationships we need to embrace that every person matters, including you. Humility is not begrudgingly going along with what everyone else wants to do because you feel you don't matter. At the same time it's not forcing others to do everything you want. If pride is an inflated view of oneself, then humility is a realistic view of oneself. You matter greatly, so much so that if you were the only human alive God would have sent His son to die for you. At the same time others matter just as much as you do.

I've found there are four crucial things we can practice to strengthen our humility.

1. Spend time with God every day. If pride causes us to think we don't need God, then humility is found when we do. James 4:10 says, "Humble yourselves before the Lord, and he will lift you up." Even when we don't feel like it, we should humble ourselves before God. I start every day reading the Bible through a plan in the app YouVersion and by praying. It's a small way to fight pride every day.
2. Admit when you are wrong by saying sorry. Proverbs 14:9 says, "Fools mock at making amends for sin, but goodwill is found among the upright." Pride hates making mistakes because it feels like there is something wrong with us. Humility allows you to see that you aren't perfect, and that's okay. Mistakes are not to be avoided but learned from.
3. Intentionally practice gratitude by thanking God every day for something you have. James 1:17 says,

"Every good and perfect gift is from above, coming down from the Father of the heavenly lights, who does not change like shifting shadows." I love the quote by Max Lucado: "What if you woke up and only had the things you thanked God for yesterday?" Gratitude fights against pride because it helps us see just how desperately we need Jesus. When we thank God, especially during the good times, it helps us not take credit for the amazing things we experience.

4. Ask for help often. Pride hates asking for help. Jerk! Humility understands that we cannot be great at everything. Intentionally asking for help keeps pride away. It's a reminder that God created us to need other people. I know this isn't easy. Proverbs 12:15 says, "The way of fools seems right to them, but the wise listen to advice." I do not feel old except for when new technology comes out. A few years ago everyone I knew under thirty was on the social media app Snapchat. I didn't get it. It was confusing and seemed silly to me. I knew that if I asked for help from someone younger than I was, they would make an old-person joke. They did. And that's okay. I'm not defined by what others say. With a little humility I was quickly shown how to use Snapchat. I was still confused afterward. I'm good at other things. My point is that asking for help is a way to practice humility.

In Jesus we can kill the jerk, but in our pride, we won't allow Him to help us. Humility allows us to understand that we cannot change or control other people. We can only work on ourselves. When a problem arises in a relationship, we must have the humility to respond with grace instead of react in anger. My hope is that when we intentionally practice humility, we can truly see ourselves and others as Jesus does.

I don't know who needs this, but there is someone reading and your pride has caused you to avoid addressing a difficult situation. You want to seek help, but pride keeps you from it. Don't wait until tomorrow. Take a step right now toward help.

Relationships often remain unbroken because one or both people are not willing to embrace humility. If you have a broken relationship, take a step toward that person now. I know it's scary, but pride is a liar and you are falling for his lies. Make a phone call now. If you cannot do that, send an e-mail. I believe in person is best because you cannot read tone, but if all you can do is message the other person, start there. Own your part. You cannot force someone else to own their part. As long as it depends on you, bring peace to the relationship.

Maybe you need to swallow your pride and confess to someone. Maybe shame has made you go into hiding. Don't let shame win. Speaking of winning…

This chapter's Win: To destroy pride, humble yourself by seeking God first. Come up with an intentional reminder to help you seek God first. Whether it's marking it in your calendar or making a note for yourself, put a reminder somewhere you'll see it in order to remind yourself to seek God first.

Questions for Further Reflection

1. What stood out to you the most in this chapter?
2. What are the two types of pride?
3. Out of the four ways to practice humility, which one seems the easiest? Which one seems the most difficult?
4. When have you seen the negative effects of pride?
5. What is one thing that you have resisted asking for help with?
6. Based on this chapter, what is God telling you to do next?

CHAPTER 11

Shame Is a Jerk

We all have a jerk within. That's been made clear at this point. Scripture teaches that all of us have sinned and fallen short of God's standards. We all have. The interesting thing about the jerk within is that it's often fueled by hurt. When we are hurting, we are not the best version of ourselves. This is where shame comes in. Shame stems from pain and leads us to allow the inner jerk to shine. Hurt people hurt people, and so much of our personal hurt comes from shame.

Shame is often mistaken for guilt, but they are not the same thing. A little guilt is healthy. Guilt can lead you to say, "I'm sorry." Guilt can lead you to make a change.

Guilt is feeling bad for something you've done.

This is not a bad thing. In fact, when we don't feel guilt it's a warning sign. Guilt can be turned to something good because you feel bad for what you've done, and therefore, you are more likely to change. Shame on the other hand is a monster. Shame is...

Shame is feeling bad for who you are.

Do you see the difference? Guilt is what I feel after I make a mistake. Shame is feeling like I am the mistake. Shame stunts our growth and leads to so many other issues. I'm convinced one of the reasons why we allow other people's opinions to impact us so much is because of the shame we feel. For example, how would you feel if I looked you in the eyes and said, "I don't like blue skin. And you have blue skin. I hate your blue skin! Your blue skin looks ridiculous!" Now, are you offended by this? Unless you are a Smurf, I think it's safe to assume you were not offended. If you were offended, then change the color of skin to neon green. Don't miss the point. If I insult you about a color of your skin that is not the color of your skin it does not bother you. Why not? Because it's not true! The insults and comments that hurt us are so often the ones that we already believe about ourselves. Don't skip by that too quickly. The insults that hurt us the most are the ones that confirm what we already believe about ourselves. Shame tells us we are not good enough, and so when someone gives the right insult, it validates how we already feel about ourselves.

This is so interesting to me because I get insulted a decent amount. I don't like that I do, but if you try to do anything, you'll be insulted. Even if you were perfect, someone would crucify you. That's a great title for a book. Someone should write that book (wink, wink). I've written books, I'm on social media a lot, I'm a pastor, and I used to blog. The bigger something is, the more criticism it will get. I'm a little peon and have still had my fair share of criticism. I can only fathom what a celebrity goes through. I've had blogs dedicated to tearing me down, critical reviews of my writing, negative posts on social media, Claymates (Season 2 of *American*

Idol runner-up Clay Aiken's fans) vow to boycott me and my church, and anonymous e-mails written by people who really don't like me. There are multiple times where insults have zero effect on me. I don't like being insulted, but the insults hold no truth over me. If I haven't hurt anyone intentionally and they aren't willing to work on the issue, then I move on. Sometimes. Other times an insult hits me so hard I can't shake it for days.

When I received my first negative book review, I realized why it hit me so hard. I was insecure about my writing. Almost all the reviews I had received were from people I knew. They know me and like me, so I felt like they were generous with their reviews. I did have one relative give me a four out of five-star review. When I asked why she didn't give five stars, she said, "When I compared your book to the classics like *The Great Gatsby* and *Pride and Prejudice* and William Shakespeare, I didn't think it was to their level." Thanks, Mom. By the way, once I explained the purpose of five-star reviews, she quickly put up a new five-star review. Which only furthers my point: people that knew me gave me high reviews to help my book get recognition. The first negative review I received for my book was from a stranger. He had no tie to me, so he was writing his honest opinion. He didn't like my book. He liked the title but felt the book was juvenile. That left me feeling insecure. I was already doubting my ability, and now someone I didn't know confirmed my doubts. When we feel shameful about who we are and others confirm our worst fears, it hits hard. Until we change how we view ourselves, we will allow other's words to destroy us. This stranger should have no space in my life. We aren't friends. He doesn't want a relationship. He didn't offer anything helpful to improve my writing. He is a guy somewhere that didn't resonate with my book. That's okay. That's fine!

It just so happened that his comment confirmed what I was already afraid of. That is a form of shame. Shame feeds off insecurity.

A lot of the time people don't mean to criticize or insult. It just happens. Some people are accidental jerks. It's like this church sign I once saw. It was not supposed to be funny, but it was.

> Do you know what Hell is?
> Come hear our preacher.

That sign was funny to everyone, but the preacher. When we live from shame we allow the words of others to define us. When someone says anything that supports the negative view we already have it can crush us. It shouldn't, but if we don't know who we are in Jesus it can.

Often I just brush off a negative comment. I believe hurt people hurt people, so I just brush it off. But sometimes the words leave a mark. For example, one of the hats I have to wear is being a boss. I've worked hard over the years to try and become the best boss I can. Being a boss is a lot like being a parent. It's a lot of work and not a lot of appreciation. Like I've never had one of my kids say, "You are a good dad." I know my kids love me, and I love the relationship with them. Come to think of it, I don't recall telling my parents they did a good job. It's just not something that comes up regularly. Mom and Dad, if you read this, please know you are great parents! My point is, it's easy to neglect to compliment someone you are close to. It's part of that honeymoon phase. We take for granted that those close to us know how we feel. They don't.

It's true with friends and family, and it's true with employees. Three years ago, I called a meeting with someone to talk to them about some behaviors that needed to change. Somehow in the meeting it got flipped around to me and what a bad boss I am. I left that meeting so confused because I called it to talk about their poor attitude and I left apologizing. Afterward I thought, *Why did I apologize?* Why did I care so much about what this person said? It's because I want to be a great leader, but I'm afraid I'm not even good. Shame is feeling bad for who you are. All of us feel shame about something. It may be harder to find for some of us, but there is an area in our life where we feel like we are just not good enough.

Shame is such a scary monster that we often ignore it by self-medicating or filling our lives with busyness. Shame is a monster because it lives in isolation and darkness. We have to get the monster out in the open. As long as it's a secret, as long as it's hidden, this monster is powerful. As long as shame is a part of your life, you will not find freedom, and the inner jerk will thrive.

Thankfully, Scripture speaks into this. The weapon to fight against shame is forgiveness. This is so crucial to understanding God's love, but many people never experience His love because shame tells them they can't. Look at what Scripture says,

> Godly sorrow brings repentance that leads to salvation and leaves no regret, but worldly sorrow brings death. (2 Cor. 7:10)

As long as shame is a part of your life, you'll never truly be free. Godly sorrow brings repentance. Repentance means to turn in the opposite direction. Godly sorrow leads to salvation. We feel godly sorrow when we reflect on our sin. Following Jesus always leads to love, but it also leads to having sin exposed. If you follow Jesus, get ready to have your feelings hurt. I believe Jesus is truthful with us because he sees our potential. Like a great coach Jesus knows what we are capable of and will call us out when we do not live up to our potential. Being in the presence of Jesus leads to repentance, but there is no shame in it. It's a holy conviction that leads to repentance.

You see, godly sorrow says, "I can't do this, but God can!" God is the one who can forgive me. But worldly sorrow brings death. That's shame. Shame is a horrible monster that wants to kill us. Shame is feeling horrible for who you are. It's feeling less than.

Shame is powerful. So powerful it leads us to go into hiding. It is highly correlated with addiction, depression, violence, aggression, bullying, suicide, and eating disorders. When shame is felt in secret, the natural response is a quick relief. Even if it's unhealthy we need something to quickly take away the sting of shame.

According to author and researcher Brené Brown, the voice of shame says two things.

Shame says:

1. You are not good enough.
2. Who are you to try?

This is the monster of shame's voice. "You are not good enough," and if we can somehow ignore this voice, it follows it up with "Who are you to try?" Shame says you've been like this for so long you'll never change. Shame says this is what you deserve.

Once you understand the monster of shame, you will see it everywhere. The monster of shame has its claws in us, and so we therefore often speak the voice of shame to others.

Using shame is a jerk move, and yet it's so ingrained in us we don't see it. We say things like, "Why are you the way that you are?" That's shame. We often parent through shame. When a kid cries, we say things like, "Don't be such a baby." That's shaming and so unhealthy. Listen, I get it. Parenting is not for the faint of heart. As a parent you play a major role in the way a kid feels about themselves. Instead of shaming our kids, we have to lead them. Call out the behavior and let them know they are better than that.

Not too long ago, we took our kids to Disney World. It was an amazing experience. When we were flying home and we were all exhausted, my son asked for us to buy him something at the airport. My son started having a meltdown because we wouldn't buy him an Iron Man stuffed toy from the airport store. It was overpriced by $12. We could buy three of the same at a store not located in the airport. It was a selfish moment. Everything in me wanted to say, "You selfish brat! We just spent a bazillion dollars on you at the happiest place in the world. We just bought you multiple stuffed animals, *and as much as I love the fact that you want a superhero, I'm not buying you anything else ever because of your attitude*!" That's what I wanted to say, but that's not helpful. We called out the bad behavior by saying, "Hayden, you are acting selfish, but you are better than this. You are not selfish. We need you to think about all the great things you got on this trip. Sit in silence and think about what you have received. Find your happy heart before we get on the plane." It took a few moments, and some patience, but it was so worth it. My son found his happy heart and was amazing on the flight home. As parents we have to separate bad behavior from who our kids are. We have to do the same thing with our friends, coworkers, neighbors, and relatives. Sometimes we have to do this for ourselves. No matter if it's kids, employees, or friends, it is difficult to correct bad behavior. A key is to separate bad behavior from the person's identity. When a person is acting like a jerk, it's important to tell ourselves that they are not a jerk. They are acting like one. They are letting their inner jerk win, but somewhere in who they are is a kind person. They may have forgotten. Let's remind them who they truly are.

When I discipline my kids, I remind them who they are. The phrase I use is, "You are better than this behavior." It shows the behavior is not acceptable but at the same time calls out their potential. Discipline is not easy, but it's so important. We discipline in love. We try to not discipline when our emotions are big. When we don't discipline, we show that we do not believe the person is any better than the bad behavior.

I don't like to be corrected, but I love when others believe in me. When we call out their potential, we show others who they could be instead of dwelling on who they currently are. When we use shame to correct, we highlight the worst about those we love. Shame is a horrible monster that has such a hold on us that we often shame others and not even know it. So think about how this can impact your spiritual life. God is love, and yet shame says, "I'm not worthy of that love." Shame says, "God can forgive everyone else but not what I've done."

The Gospel Destroys Shame

Shame holds us back and holds us down. This is why the Gospel is so powerful. The word *gospel* means good news. It's what Jesus brought. In fact, the first four books of the New Testament are called the Gospels because it's the good news story of Jesus.

The gospel of Jesus says:

1. You are not good enough, but God is.
2. Who are you to try? You are God's child!

The gospel doesn't lie to you and say you are perfect. The gospel speaks directly to your shame. You are not worthy but God is. Way too many Christians think the gospel is the starting point of faith. That is, they understand they are a sinner, say a prayer, and become a Christian. To way too many Christians that's the gospel, but that's only the tip of the gospel iceberg. The gospel is what it's all about. You are not good enough, but God is. That's the gospel. You are not good enough to overcome your issue, but God is. You are not good enough, but Jesus is. This is why…

Big Idea: The antidote to shame is forgiveness.

This is the gospel. The good news is that unconditional forgiveness is offered through Jesus. Shame lies to you and says you cannot be forgiven, but Jesus is truth and the truth will set you free.

> If we confess our sins, he is faithful and just and will forgive us our sins and purify us from all unrighteousness. (1 John 1:9)

God forgives! Shame is a liar that will tell you what you've done is bigger than who God is. Shame will tell you that you aren't worthy of this type of love. We cannot out sin the love of God. God doesn't love you more when you are good, and He doesn't love you less when you are bad. You may not be worthy of love, but that didn't stop Jesus from dying for you. When you confess your sins to God, He is faithful and will forgive you. Then shame starts to lose its grip. My prayer is that today you will understand God's love and release the grip shame has. Shame tells you not to try, but I'm praying that you will have a supernatural surge of courage to accept the love of God.

To Remove Shame Don't Stop at God's Forgiveness

Many people never receive God's forgiveness. Many do, but unfortunately, this is where a lot of people stop. If you are a Christian, then you may understand God's forgiveness and still struggle with shame. I want to show you why. Scripture is clear: we go to God for forgiveness, but we are to go to God's people for healing.

> Therefore confess your sins to each other and pray for each other so that you may be healed. The prayer of a righteous person is powerful and effective. (James 5:16)

Did you catch what that verse said? Confess your sins to each other so that you'll be healed. This is where so many Christians fall short. We are forgiven by Jesus, but you can be forgiven and still beat down by shame. Shame tells us to keep it a secret. Shame tells us that we can work on our issues by ourselves. Shame tells us that no one will understand. Shame is a jerk! We are only as healthy as our secrets. The key to finding freedom is confession. Find someone safe and start the journey of healing. It is scary, but it's so worth it.

Shame thrives in secrecy, silence, and judgment.

This can be especially difficult for men. For men shame is "don't let me seem weak." We feel the need to be strong. Think about this. We often shame boys into being strong, saying things like, "Don't cry like a girl." That's a horrible statement. First off, it's insulting to girls. Second off, showing emotion is not weakness. It takes great strength to be vulnerable. In fact, it's been noted that when we cry it's a way for the soul to show us what is really important. That's why I don't apologize for crying. If I cry it's because it's important. I don't apologize for having emotions and feeling feelings. The voice of shame lies and says that guys have to be strong. Sometimes the strongest thing you can do is ask for help.

Shame for women often comes from feeling like you have to do it all, do it perfectly, and never let them see you sweat. There is a picture in many woman's mind of living up to the image of Superwoman. The problem is you are not perfect. And your imperfections become fuel for shame when you keep them to yourself. Often women feel overwhelmed with the amount of responsibilities they have. In marriage, often women gain an animosity toward their husband because of all the responsibilities they are juggling. The belief that a woman has to be Wonder Woman is killing a lot of women. It's leading them to not ask for help and then feel shameful for not being able to handle everything. Sometimes the strongest thing you can do is ask for help.

Not Everyone Can Handle Your Story

One of the reasons we keep shameful things to ourselves is because not everyone is safe. We have been shamed. We have been judged. We have been hurt by others. There are safe people out there, but it takes some work to find them. Being authentic is incredibly important, but it doesn't mean sharing everything with everyone. We must share our struggles of shame with someone if we want to kill the jerk, but we also need to know the person we share with is safe. I love what Brené Brown says:

> Our stories are not meant for everyone. Hearing them is a privilege, and we should always ask ourselves this before we share: "Who has earned the right to hear my story?" If we have one or two people in our lives who can sit with us and hold space for our shame stories, and love us for our strengths and struggles, we are incredibly lucky. If we have a friend, or small group of friends, or family who embraces our imperfections, vulnerabilities, and power, and fills us with a sense of belonging, we are incredibly lucky.

The church should be the safest place on the planet because we have a Savior who doesn't shame us. Unfortunately, the church isn't always the safest place. We should not blindly assume that just because someone calls themselves Christian they are safe. Even in the church you should search for those who are safe. We all need a safe place. A place where we can confess our sins one to another. You can be forgiven and not healed from shame. To be shame free, you need confession. This is why small groups are so crucial in church. We need safe places where we can be real. The truth is not everyone can handle our junk. But someone can.

To defeat the monster of shame:

- Go to God for forgiveness
- Go to God's people for healing

When we struggle and share it with someone and they give us judgment, it confirms what shame tells us, that we are broken. When we share with someone and they say, "Me too," it feels like a weight is lifted off. We all struggle, but you don't have to struggle alone. Scripture is clear: we go to God for forgiveness, and we go to God's people for healing.

You will never change outside of relationships.

We are only as healthy as our secrets. The key to finding freedom is confession. Find someone safe and start the journey to healing. It is scary but so worth it. Every recovery group knows this. We need safe people to confess to, and we need community to keep us accountable for our decisions. Somehow we have relegated groups for major addictions. Change happens in relationships. You don't have to wait until you are at the end of your rope to be in community. When we feel safe to be ourselves and at the same time are loved to become who God says we are, we change. Maybe we should start a Jerks Anonymous. Hi, my name is Rob and I'm a recovering Jerk.

If you don't have someone safe to talk to, find someone. If there is no one, I recommend seeing a Christian counselor. How can you tell if someone is safe? Are they willing to share their struggles? When someone constantly pretends to be perfect, it's a good sign they haven't wrestled with their sins. When someone is authentic and open about their struggles, there is a great chance they are safe. It doesn't mean they are perfect, but you aren't looking for perfection. You've found perfection in Jesus. He has already forgiven you. What you are looking for is freedom. Forgiveness comes from God, but freedom comes from confessing to God's people.

This chapter's Win: To defeat the monster of shame, confess to God for forgiveness and to one of God's people for healing.

Questions for Further Reflection

1. What was your biggest takeaway from this chapter?
2. What is the difference between guilt and shame?
3. Who is the safest person you know?
4. Where do you see shame the most?
5. How can the church become a safe place to share shameful feelings?
6. Who do you know that might be a safe person for you to find healing in the form of confession?

CHAPTER 12

Trust vs. Suspicion

Sometimes we are accidental jerks. Our intentions are good, but it doesn't change the fact that we still acted like a jerk. It's like the one time someone came up to me after a sermon and said, "I don't normally like it when you preach, but today was actually good." Somewhere in there was a compliment. I was not offended by the statement. My preaching doesn't have to be everyone's cup of tea. I'm thankful that on that day God spoke through me to this person. I am not throwing stones at this person because I've done the same type of thing a multitude of times. My intentions were good, but I fumbled the delivery. My intentions were good, but I still hurt someone. We are all way more sensitive than we want to admit and at times more insensitive than we should be.

Often when our feelings get hurt it's not because the other person is intentionally trying to be a jerk. It's because people play by different rules and learning a new set of rules isn't easy. The issue comes when someone breaks one of our rules and in turn we think, *They did it on purpose*. Maybe. But we have to leave room for a maybe not. If you have someone who is intentionally breaking your rules, you need to set up a boundary. The truth is, the people we love, love us back. When they break one of our rules, we have to decide if they did it on purpose or if it's a simple mistake.

If you want less drama in your relationships, start practicing to believe the best about people. When someone breaks one of your rules, you get to decide if they did it on purpose or not. No one else gets to make this decision. You have to make sure that you believe the best, and by deciding to believe they did not break one of your rules on purpose is believing the best.

It's not fair to judge someone else's intentions. When someone does something that you don't like, your mind has a way of putting them on trial. You start to analyze and think about what they did. And that point you start to come up with conclusions about why they did what they did. I love the definition of judgment by Dr. James B. Richards. He says,

> A judgment is when we attach a "why" to someone's actions.

All humans are wired to do this. We attach a why to someone else's actions. We think we know why they did what they did. We think, *He did that on purpose because he is selfish*. We think, *She did that on purpose because she is so mean*. You cannot see someone else's motives. You have to ask, unearth, and discover someone's motives. I love what Brendan Manning says about this:

> None of us has ever seen a motive. Therefore, we don't know we can't do anything more than suspect what inspires the action of another. For this good and valid reason, we're told not to judge.

> Tragedy is that our attention centers on what people are not, rather than on what they are and who they might become.

When we do not ask questions, we often assume what the other person is feeling. That's unfair and unhealthy. We often allow differences to define how we feel about someone.

Here is a key when it comes to other people: believe the best. Simply assume that the person you are in relationship with isn't out to get you. Often when we are offended, hurt, or just disappointed we assume the worst. For example, did the person you are in relationship with wake up today and form a plot to ruin your day? Are they James Bond villain? Is their first thought of the day, *What am I going to do today? Try and take over the world?*

Here's what you can decide: is the person you are in relationship with an evil monster? If so, you need to separate yourself from them. My guess is, for most of us the person who we are upset with is not a monster. They have unintentionally broken one of our rules, and because the rules are so ingrained in us, we can't fathom why they would do that. The only explanation is they are the worst. You cannot control other people. You can only work on controlling yourself. Choosing to believe the best is a major step into having healthy relationships.

Remember, when it comes to conflict, we all naturally respond in one of three ways. We are either passive, passive-aggressive, or aggressive. That's natural, but God is supernatural and gives us the ability to respond instead of react to conflict.

After teaching on this at my church, I received the following text: "Wrote an e-mail with a super passive-aggressive paragraph. Removed said paragraph. Sent e-mail. I don't feel better but know it's right. I blame you and the Holy Spirit, and my husband for telling me I can't say those things. Jesus help." That's glorious! When I asked if I could share this response, she said I could and then followed up. She said the person she sent the e-mail to responded to her and it was a super great e-mail. She said, "The passive-aggressive paragraph would have most likely changed her view of me. Glad I kept it out."

That's what I'm talking about! We are cannot control other people; we can only work on controlling ourselves. I'm responsible for my responses.

This chapter is about the importance of believing the best in a relationship. The Scripture that is going to guide this is a very famous verse. In fact, five out of every four weddings use this verse. This verse is written by the apostle Paul. He wrote a letter to the church in Corinth because they were all kinds of jacked up. One of the things they were fighting about was spiritual gifts. Some were looking down at others because they didn't have certain spiritual gifts. Paul says, I don't care if you have the most amazing gift in the world. If it's void of love, then it is a resounding gong or clanging cymbal. Another way to say this is you can be right and still be wrong. If you are right about something but don't have love, then you are just adding to the noise. He then thankfully defines what love is. This is helpful because love can mean so many different things. I feel love for chipotle and love for my kids. Even though a chipotle burrito looks like a cute little swaddled baby, the love I have for this food is very different than the love I have for my kids. When my kids were babies and swaddled nicely like a chipotle burrito, I was never tempted to take a bite out of them. Because love can be broad, Paul gives us the defining qualities of what it means to love someone. In this we see that love and trust go together. Paul writes,

> Love does not delight in evil but rejoices with the truth. It always protects, always trusts, always hopes, always perseveres. (1 Cor. 13:6–7)

Have you ever wondered why the people closest to you get on your nerves more so than others? Sure you love your family more than you love others, but isn't it true that they get on our nerves, irk us, annoy us, and make us more angry than other people? There is some science to why that is. Remember the honeymoon phase mentioned in chapter 1? The honeymoon phase is more than for just married couples. In all relationships we experience a honeymoon phase. The honeymoon phase is that period of time where we are on our best behavior. So this is when you first start your job and you work harder and try harder in order to make a good impression. For example, if you are typically late to everything, for a brand-new job you'll make sure that you are on time. This may happen in friendship. When a friendship is new, you'll work really hard to win the other person over. We see this often in dating. When a couple starts dating, they don't lead with their worst. When a couple starts dating, they lead with their best in an attempt to win the other person over. So this is where the guy pulls out all the romantic stops and the girl never gets a headache before they start making out. This honeymoon period is based on the fear of having someone leave. We are the best versions of ourselves because we want others to accept us. When a relationship is new and exciting, our bodies have an increase in nerve growth factor, which increases the feeling of connection.

Now, on average, the honeymoon period lasts two years. Could be shorter or longer but on average it's about two years. Once the relationship is no longer new and a little less exciting, we start to exit the honeymoon phase. There is even more to this though. The reason the honeymoon period ends is because we no longer fear that the other person is going to leave us. So the good side of this is that once the honeymoon period ends, we are our true selves. So the people we are closest to see a silly side that we may not show anyone else. The unfortunate part about the honeymoon phase is that once it ends, we naturally start to take the other person for granted. So when a couple first starts dating, he is on his best behavior and remembers to put the toilet seat down. When he does forget, she thinks, *That's so cute. I love it when he forgets.* Once we exit the honeymoon phase, the other person's shortcomings are no longer cute. It's like the saying, "In dating opposites attract, but in marriage opposites attack." We get annoyed, and because we no longer fear the other may leave, we let them know it. So once we lose the fear that we might lose the job, friendship, or family member, then our true selves come out. This is the jerk inside all of us.

When it comes to relationships, if you and I are not intentional, we do damage to our relationships. A person can extend the honeymoon phase by going on dates, doing nice things for the other person, or intentionally investing in someone. A little work goes a long way. The problem is if we are not intentional, we will take the other person for granted.

Once you become comfortable with someone, you naturally move from believing the best to believing the worst. At the beginning of the relationship you gave them the benefit of the doubt, but once the honeymoon phase is over, there is no doubt they are annoying and you need to correct them. This is important! It's important because when you exit the honeymoon phase, you will start to take things personally. This is when you start to believe that the only reason they would do what they just did was to intentionally hurt you. This is why relationships are so tough. We literally have to fight against nature. So when Paul writes about love he makes it clear that love is not a feeling. Love is a choice. Look at what Paul says,

> *Love does not delight in evil but rejoices with the truth.*

This is a choice. If I choose to love, then I am not going to delight in evil, but instead I am going to rejoice in truth. Another translation of this word *evil* is the word *iniquity*. So another way to look at this verse is to say love does not delight in sin. Now, in English we only have one word for *sin*. The New Testament part of the Bible was written in Greek, and there are thirty-three Greek words for *sin*. Two of the main ones stand in contrast to each other. One means to miss the mark. It's a picture of archery. Where you were aiming at the mark but you fell short. This is like if you decided you wanted to cuss less and you started working on not cussing. You found ways to use substitute cuss words like "Shut the front door" or "What the Hellman's Mayonnaise." You are feeling pretty good about yourself until you stub your innocent little pinky toe on a coffee table. Before you know it swears are pouring out of your mouth, "*Fudge*!" But you didn't say *fudge* (See the classic Christmas movie *A Christmas Story* for this reference). Afterward you would say to yourself, "I missed the mark." I was trying my best, and I fell short. It wasn't intentional. We've all made mistakes like this. We didn't mean to, but we still did it. Thank God for grace. We are all works in progress.

Contrast that with another Greek word for *sin* that means to deliberately climb on the other side of the fence. This is the mind-set that you don't care what God's standards are, you are going to intentionally sin. It's when a person thinks, *Tonight I'm going to get all sorts of wasted* or *I'm going to hurt them and I don't care what God says.* Fill in the blank with whatever bad choice there is. This is where you are looking to make a bad decision.

Now, our verse says love does not delight in evil, but a better word for that would be *iniquity*. The iniquity it's talking about here is more so the kind of sin that is deliberate. Love does not take delight in deliberate sin. Instead, our hearts should break. Now what does this have to do with you and your relationships? That's a great question. Thanks for asking it. Paul says love does not delight in evil but rejoices with truth. So we have to combine these two ideas.

When it comes to your relationships, whenever you feel hurt, wounded, or offended, the natural response is believe that the person that hurt you did it on purpose. Right? Like if the person in my life truly loved me, they wouldn't have hurt me that way. We are naturally born to believe the worst. It's an entitlement thing. I see this often with my kids. One of my kids will accidentally bump the other, and they will declare, "He hit me on purpose!" No, I saw the whole thing. On this occasion he just accidentally bumped you.

In psychology this is called fundamental attribution error. I mentioned this in chapter 7. It's important enough to revisit here. It is the tendency to attribute the negative or frustrating behaviors of people to their intentions and personalities. So when someone doesn't meet our expectations, this error leads us to believe that it is something that is fundamentally wrong with their personality or character. We think, *She was late because she is lazy*. In other words when someone doesn't meet our expectations, we think it's because there is something fundamentally wrong with the other person. On the other hand, when we do something wrong, we attribute it to environmental issues. We think, *I am late because traffic was bad.* You know traffic wasn't the real cause. In this case you left late and there just happened to be enough cars to justify you saying there is traffic. If you left early enough, you would not have been late. Or something to that degree. Can you smell what I'm cooking? You cut yourself slack but not others. In relationships this is where we say, "He said that because he doesn't love me." Or we say, "She did that because she was trying to hurt me."

Whenever we feel hurt or disappointment, we naturally react. To kill the jerk, you are going to work on responding instead of reacting. Hurt people hurt people. So when the people closest to us hurt us, we have to rejoice with the truth. What's the truth?

"The people that truly love me do not intentionally try to hurt me. I am hurt, but that does not mean they did it on purpose."

Now, where this goes out the window is someone in your life is literally hurting you. You should not be in a relationship where someone hits you, verbally abuses you, or sexually abuses you in any way. If that's the case you need to separate yourself from the person. That's what the verse says. Don't delight in evil. Call out evil. Reject evil. Don't go along with evil.

If the other person is not intentionally hurting you, then in order to have a healthy relationship you must choose to believe the best. When someone in your life upsets you, you get to choose how your respond. Is the person who just hurt me evil and truly trying to hurt me or are they generally good-natured? So the next time you are hurt by someone you love, ask yourself, "Did they intentionally wake us this morning and say today I'm going to hurt you?" That's an evil person.

Behind every healthy relationship is the choice to believe the best.

This isn't natural, but it's so helpful. When I feel hurt, I have to rejoice with the truth. What's the truth? The truth is, if the person is my family, friend, neighbor, or coworker and they truly love me, they aren't intentionally trying to hurt me. They might have hurt me. It might be because they had a bad day, were grumpy, lacked sleep, were hungry, where unintentionally hurt by me, or who knows what else. If they hurt me, it's either because they didn't mean to or because they are hurting within.

We have to learn to respond instead of react to hurt. If hurt people hurt people, then when someone in your life hurts, you it's a sign they are hurting. How should you respond to hurt? With healing! Once the honeymoon phase ends, we naturally respond to hurt with more hurt. We are way more sensitive then we like to admit. Once you establish that you are on the same team and that other person isn't intentionally trying to hurt you, then you will be able to respond to their hurt with healing. That brings us to the big idea of this chapter.

Big Idea: I will choose to believe that you aren't trying to be a jerk.

Now if the people in your life are evil and they wake up every morning like a James Bond villain trying to plot a way to destroy you, then you have an issue. More likely the people in your life are not intentionally trying to hurt you, annoy you, bother you. Once you believe the best, then you get to choose how to respond. When I feel hurt, I will choose to bring healing. Look at what Paul says next:

> It always protects, always trusts, always hopes, always perseveres.

So when it comes to love, love is a choice. And when I am hurt, I must choose to bring love. Love always protects. Why is this important? Because when you feel hurt by your relationships, the natural reaction is to try and hurt them back. That's not love! Love is a choice to believe the best. If the person isn't evil, then you have to choose to believe that they didn't mean to hurt you. Love does not delight in evil but rejoices in truth!

Four Ways to Bring Healing to Your Relationships

This is easier said than done. I get it. I don't always get this right, but the following has helped me have healthy relationships by believing the best.

Four ways to bring healing to your relationships:

1. When I am hurt, I will protect you by remembering we are on the same team.
2. When I am hurt, I trust that you didn't mean to hurt me.

3. When I am hurt, I will hope that we can solve this together.
4. When I am hurt, I will persevere by working to solve the problem.

This is not easy, but it's so crucial. When you feel hurt, the natural reaction is to hurt back. That's not healthy. When I believe the best and trust that you are not my enemy, you are not trying to hurt me. When you didn't do the dishes, it wasn't an attempt to hurt me. When you didn't meet my needs, it wasn't an attempt to hurt me. When you acted in a way that was different than me, it was not an attempt to hurt me. I am hurt, but I am going to believe that you didn't mean to. Once I get this down, then I am at a place to bring healing to the hurt. But until you convince yourself that the people in your life aren't out to get you, you will always react to hurt instead of responding.

When I Am Hurt, I Will Protect You

When I am hurt, I will protect you by remembering we are on the same team. When someone says something hurtful to you, it is a sign of brokenness. To respond to hurt with hurt does not fix the situation. I will protect you by working on myself. When I'm feeling hurt, I will express it in a healthy way. I will refuse to be passive, passive-aggressive, or aggressive. I will communicate using "I" instead of "You" statements. I will believe the best about you. I will treat you the way I want to be treated, not how I'm feeling.

When I Am Hurt, I Will Trust

When I am hurt, I will trust that you didn't mean to hurt me. I will do this expressing my hurt in a helpful way. Asking questions is a great way to respond to hurt. It's a way to assume the best and de-escalate the conflict. For example, after someone has said something hurtful to you, reply, "That hurt. I know you don't mean to hurt me. Did I do something unintentionally to hurt you?" Other questions to ask can include, "Can you help me understand that?" "This seems to be something you are passionate about. What is your passion around this?" "Can you tell me why this doesn't work for you?" When you are hurt, it's so important to remember the goal of communication. The goal of communication is understanding, not agreement. Seek to understand by asking questions. You might just find that the other person didn't mean to hurt you.

When I Am Hurt, I Will Hope

Believing the best happens when we have hope. I hope that things will work out. I hope that we can figure this out. I hope that we can solve this together. You can either fight in a relationship or for a relationship. When you establish some rules of engagement, then you can solve problems together. The rules of engagement help keep the jerk at bay and ensure that the problem is actually being worked on. We are better together. In conflict we have to have hope that we can figure out the solution together.

When I Am Hurt, I Will Persevere

In all relationships you will get hurt. Even if it's not intentional hurt will happen. When it does, I will choose to persevere. Again, this is not being a victim or allowing oneself to be physically or emotionally hurt. This is a perseverance to find a solution. It may be a rough season, but we can make it through it. In order to do so, we need to have some relationship optimism. It may take going to see a counselor to solve the issue. It may take reading another book that can help unlock the answer. It may take a few weeks or months, but I believe we can make it through this. I'm not going to throw in the towel. I won't run away when things get tough. I'm going to run to you. I'm going to pursue you during difficult seasons.

Let's Wrap This Up

All relationships have issues. A big one is constantly believing that when someone hurts you it is on purpose. If the other person truly loves you, then they aren't out to get you. It may feel like they are, but remember you are to treat others like you want to be treated. In the same way you have to choose to believe the best the other people your life have to do the same thing for you. When you hurt someone, don't you want them to believe it wasn't on purpose? If you are not a James Bond villain and don't want other viewing you like that, then remember to not treat others that way. It helps to literally say out loud, "I will choose to believe that you aren't trying to hurt me." Say it to yourself in your mind. Say it out loud. Tattoo it on your forearm to see it regularly. I'm not trying to tell you what to do. You can decide if and how you want to remember this. The point is that without believing the best, it is impossible to have healthy relationships.

At this point you may be asking, "But what if they are intentionally trying to hurt me?" What do we do when someone we love lashes out by being passive, passive-aggressive, or aggressive? We believe the best that says the only reason they are doing this is because they are hurting. We apply chapter 2 and treat them how we would want to be treated. We communicate expectations. We take a time-out to remove ourselves from an unhealthy situation. We don't allow someone's bad behavior to change who we are.

There are times where the people closest to us may hurt us on purpose. It is because they are hurting. This doesn't justify it. Just remember that tit for tat doesn't work. Evil for evil doesn't bring healing. A person you love may have a temporary lapse, but when they truly love you, they will see the error of their ways and repent.

Telling yourself that the person who hurt you didn't mean to hurt you can help talk you off the ledge. I know. I practice this often. Sometimes I mess this up, and when I do, I repent. I've come so far in learning how to respond to the hurt I feel. For so long it was easy for me to bark at the people closest to me whenever I felt hurt. Now I've practiced saying, "______ is not evil, so I have to trust that he/she didn't mean to hurt me." It's helped me respond with grace, have healthy conversations, and see growth in my relationships. I believe it can have the same impact for you.

This chapter's Win: Practice believing the best about your relationships. Write down, "If ________ is not evil, then I have to trust they didn't mean to hurt me." When you feel hurt, communicate by bringing healing.

Questions for Further Reflection

1. When have you believed something only to later find out it wasn't true?
2. Which one of the four ways to bring healing to your relationship do you struggle to provide naturally?
3. Which one is the easiest for you to do?
4. Is there someone you have turned into a James Bond villain when in all actuality they are a good-natured person?
5. If so is there something you need to ask forgiveness for?
6. What can you do to remember to believe the best?

CHAPTER 13

There Is No Time to Be a Jerk

We all have an inner jerk, and for many people we feel like in time the jerk will go away. Unfortunately, that's not true. Time does not change who you are, it reveals who you are. That is, we don't get better with time unless we are intentional. What you struggle with now is the same thing you'll struggle with later unless you intentionally address it. We think we will become better over time, but we aren't wine. We don't get to just sit around and improve. Jerks don't die easily. It takes intentional effort to take them down.

The problem is a lot of times we don't want to address our issues. In fact, sometimes we like the very things that ultimately harm us. Instant gratification is immediate pleasure with delayed consequences. It's easy to have a to-do list of things we should work on—one day.

Because we feel like there is always tomorrow, we end up putting off what we should work on today. I've heard it said, "We underestimate how much we can do in five years, and we overestimate what we can do in a year." That is we often put off what we should do because we think we can cram in life change. I know, I do this. I was in a fitness challenge, and during one of the weeks, I used the excuse of being busy to not walk my daily 10K steps. I kept saying I'll double up tomorrow. After a few days I had assumed a massive debt of steps. Putting it off until tomorrow led to trying to walking 40K steps in one day. That's twenty miles of miserable. What should have taken me a little bit of time every day ended up consuming my entire day. Not only did it add stress to my life, it also wore me slap out. Oh, and it rained on my catch-up day. I ended up doing power laps in the local mall with some serious senior adults who mall-walk like it's an Olympic competition. Oh, and I didn't even complete my goal. I fell short of my goal because who has time to walk twenty miles. I was slap tired and defeated. Defeated by some of the senior adult mall walkers. They were serious and faster than they should have been. They also gave me the stink eye when I tried to pass them.

It's not just me. We often put off what we should do in place of what we feel pressured to do. Living moment by moment allows whatever feels most immediate to take priority. I once taught a Sunday school class for sixth grade boys. I challenged them weekly to ready the Bible five days a week. One of the students was a homeschooler. He bragged about only doing school for a few hours a day but then said he didn't have time to read the Bible. I challenged him on this. It did not seem to have any impact on him. No matter what I said, he stuck to his story. That all changed one Sunday. One week we went around the circle sharing how many times we read the Bible that week. It wasn't meant to be a high pressure or stressful situation. I made it fun. I gave prizes to students, and we encouraged one another with this weekly challenge. On this week the homeschooled student proudly declared that he read the Bible five times that week. We were all blown away. We celebrated and cheered him on. After a few minutes of us all losing our minds in excitement, he let us in on a secret.

He confessed to reading the Bible five times on Friday. He crammed it all in on one day. I got a good laugh out of that. Technically, he did the work but he is illustrating an important thing we all do. We tend to cram what we should do because we prioritize what we feel. The issue is, feelings are misleading. I often feel like doing things I shouldn't do and I don't feel like doing things I should. I get to the end of a day, week, month, or year and look back and wonder where all the time went. We often say, "I don't have time for that," yet if you have time to check social media or watch Netflix, you have time. It's not a matter of not having enough; it's a matter of not prioritizing what is truly important. The following verse is so crucial for making the most out of our lives and killing the inner jerk.

> Teach us to number our days, that we may gain a heart of wisdom. (Ps. 90:12)

The verse is an amazing prayer to pray. It would be worth it to write it out, memorize it, and quote it daily. Teach us to number our days. Research has shown that without a deadline humans tend to put things off. It's a common problem at jobs. If you are given an assignment without a deadline, the chances of that assignment getting done is slim to none. A deadline, even a self-imposed deadline, drastically increases our chances of completing a goal. Statistics show that 86 percent of high school students procrastinate on assignments. Now we tend to think that we get better with age, but watch this. When students get to college, the number goes up. Eighty-eight percent of college student procrastinate on assignments. This same thing happens in marriage. A wife often will ask her husband for help fixing something around the house. If there is not a deadline, you can all but guarantee that husband will put it off. He hasn't forgotten it. He just hasn't gotten around to it yet. The mantra of husbands everywhere is, "If I say I'm going to do it, I will. You don't have to remind me every six months." Ha-ha! That's funny, not funny.

Don't Waste Your Life

The truth is…

No one wastes their life intentionally; we waste it accidentally one day at a time.

One of the biggest obstacles with life is that it's so daily. It's easy to think, *I'll change one day*. It's easy to think I'll work on that next week. It's easy to think, *One day I'll kill the jerk*. It's easy to put off life change because we feel there is always a tomorrow. What if there is no tomorrow? What if the person passes away? What if the opportunity passes us by? What if what we say we should do becomes the very thing we never do? We think we have unlimited time, but the truth is, our time is limited and we need to make the most of it. Look at what the psalmist says,

> Our days may come to seventy years, or eighty, if our strength endures; yet the best of them are but trouble and sorrow, for they quickly pass, and we fly away. (Ps. 90:10)

We have a short amount of time. During our life it can feel like each season lasts an eternity, but when we look back, we can feel like time passed us by. If you have littles at home, you know the days are long but the years are short. Before you know, this season passes you by. If you are not careful, you'll miss seasons of life. If we are lucky, we get seventy to eighty good years. If we aren't careful, life will blow by us with little to show for it. When we learn to number our days, it helps put an expiration date to our life. Not in a morbid or fearful way. It's more so in a way that helps us prioritize what is actually important.

Dr. Leslie Weatherhead calculated the average length of a life using the hours of one day to illustrate the importance of recognizing the value of time. So we know there are twenty-four hours in a day. If you look at your age, he represents age with time. He concluded:

Life by 24 Hours

If you are 15 years old the time is 10:25 a.m.
If your age is 20, the time is 11:34 a.m.
If your age is 25, the time is 12:42 p.m.
If you're 30, the time is 1:51 p.m.
If you're 35, the time is 3:00 p.m.
If you're 40 the time is 4:08 p.m.
At age 45, the time is 5:15 p.m.
If you're 50, the time is 6:25 p.m.
By age 55, the time is 7:24 p.m.
If you're 60, the time is 8:42 p.m.
If you're 65, the time is 9:51 p.m.
And if you you're 70 the time is 11 p.m.

Time is ticking away. God, teach us to number our days! So a year from now who do you want to be? In five years, who do you want to be? In ten years, who do you hope to be? Now, the tricky thing is a lot of us don't know. We don't know what our purpose is. We don't know what we would like to do. We don't know who we would like to become. We simply exist. We go from one moment to the next. When we live life without purpose, we are passive. We live life with purpose, we are active. When we don't know our purpose, we are in danger of allowing the immediate to dictate what we do. The jerk comes out when we passively let life come to us. I don't believe life is meant to simply be endured! Life is meant to be lived. Truly lived. In order to do that we have to be intentional. Look at what the verse says next:

> Teach us to number our days, that we may gain a heart of wisdom. (Ps. 90:12)

We often spend so much time doing things that don't matter on the other side of eternity. They feel really important right here and now, but later on they just feel silly. The Psalmist understood this. The prayer is not just to help me number my days. It's to help me number my days so I may gain a heart of wisdom. In the ancient Hebrew culture, wisdom is so much more than being smart. You can be smart and still be very foolish. According to the Hebrew culture, wisdom is…

Wisdom is the art of skillful living.

That's so good. Often in life we ask the wrong questions. We focus on things like "Does this feel good?" or "Is this fun?" or "Do I feel like doing this?" We so often let feelings direct our decisions. Wisdom goes beyond feelings. Based on who I want to be, what is the wise thing for me to do? Based on what I want out of my marriage, what is the wise thing to do? Based on where I want to be health wise, what is the wise thing to do? Based on what is most important in this world, how am I spending my time? I love the quote by author and speaker LysaTerKeurst.

Today's choices become tomorrow's circumstances.

Intentional Relationships Don't Happen by Accident

Now the question is, what does this have to do with relationships? It has a lot to do with them. Because we often prioritize the immediate, we put off the things in life that are truly important. We have to do things like chores, jobs, car maintenance, sleep, and eat. We often move from one event to the next feeling worn out, all the while clinging to the excuse that we don't have time. Nobody has time! We make time to do what is truly important to us. After our relationship with God, our relationship with others is the most important thing about our life. It's more important than our bank account, house, or social status. If relationships are currency, I want to be filthy rich!

Imagine with me that relationships are like a funnel, and every person you know is made up of $100 of coins. Because the world is a difficult place to live in, we are constantly having some of our coins drop out the bottom of the funnel. Just by living and by nature of the funnel we are losing a little bit every day. It may not be noticeable at first, but before long we start to feel a little depleted. In order to keep each person feeling filled, we need others to pour into us. When we don't feel full, we often let the jerk out. When desperation rises, standards fall. When we allow ourselves to feel depleted, we often lower our standards to whatever will immediately make us feel better. When our inner jerk comes out, it takes a handful of the coins from another person. Unfortunately, because the way negativity works, when we show love, it only puts back in half of the coins negativity takes out. It takes twice as much love to make up the deficit of negativity. The only way I know how to keep the funnel full is to intentionally pour into it. In fact, that's the big idea for this chapter.

Big Idea: Great relationships happen intentionally, not accidentally.

There are lots of people who want to be rich in money or rich with stuff, but I don't hear a lot of people talking about being rich relationally. We act as if once we have a relationship, we don't have to do anything. Remember the honeymoon period? It's that time in our life where the relationship is new. During this time, we put in a lot of extra work to win the other person over. We do this in friendship, romance, and with jobs. The problem is, relationships are like the funnel. With relationships we are either draining or pouring life into others.

Relationships are always in motion. We are either moving closer to or further away from those we love. There is no holding pattern. You may not be doing anything intentionally to push someone away, but are you doing something intentionally to draw closer to? Great relationships happen intentionally, not accidentally. In relationships we are either growing closer or further away. If you want great friendships, you have to become intentional at having friendships. If you want a great marriage, you have to become intentional at it. If you want a great relationship with God, you have to be intentional. Great relationships happen intentionally, not accidentally. Because time waits for no one, we have to make sure we are spending our time wisely.

This is something that many want to push back on. We don't like the thought of having to put in effort in order to have healthy relationships. We love the idea of healthy relationships naturally happening like something out of a Disney movie. We wait for the prince to just show up and rescue us. I'm convinced this is why so many people don't initiate social plans. The temptation is to wait to see who is doing what and if they will invite us. I also believe this is why some people do not have friends. We think that friendship should happen naturally. If you want a great friendship, it takes intentional effort. When you find someone you connect with, take the initiative. If you don't have anyone you connect with, expand your circle.

We like for things to just happen naturally when it comes to relationships. There is something that feels almost wrong about intentionally investing in relationships. I wonder if that comes because we often have seen others use manipulation to get what they want. Or maybe it's because we don't feel like it's authentic if it's intentional. We enjoy when we naturally have a desire to do something, and being intentional means we try to do something even when it doesn't feel natural. Many people get this with fitness and nutrition. Some get this with finances. Few get this with relationships. Great relationships happen intentionally, not accidentally. I'm truly not sure the reason, and I've never read any research to show why we want to push back on this idea. What I do know is that in every area of my life where I have success it's come intentionally, not accidentally. I don't have Jell-O soft abs on accident. I've earned my gut. Whether it's been a diet, a budget, or getting better as a leader, I've experienced success when I've been intentional in the areas I want to grow.

Great relationships happen intentionally, not accidentally.

If you have ever been hurt by relationships, if you feel you are too busy to maintain them, if you don't understand why you don't have a closer group of friends, this chapter is for you. If you feel you have a great group of friends and don't need anymore, then this chapter is for you. If you can't fathom carving out time to hang out, have fun, and enjoy the company of others, this chapter is for you. If you have ever wished you had more friends, this chapter is for you.

The early church was in a very interesting situation. The attendance was exploding despite the fact that there was severe persecution. One of the themes of the New Testament is to keep holding on. It's easy to quit in life, but true life change happens over time and in community. Scripture says,

> And let us consider how we may spur one another on toward love and good deeds. (Heb. 10:24)

Did you catch what the verse said? Let us consider how we may spur one another on toward love and good deeds. I believe in preaching. I believe in learning and reading books like this one. All of it is important, but it's only one part of how we grow. Real sustainable life change happens in community.

When I'm strong I'm really strong, but when I get weak, I'm pathetically weak. All humans have moments of weakness. The verse says that you need to hold on to the hope we profess, but then the next verse says that we need to spur one another on. How do you spur someone on? By leading yourself well while living in community with others who lead themselves well.

It's so easy when you get around other people to want to change them. But people aren't changed by having their faults pointed out. You spur people on by the way you live your life. In turn you are spurred on by others when they lead themselves well. Specifically, it says spur others on by love and good deeds. Lives aren't changed when we argue theology online. Lives are changed by love and good deeds that point to God.

Let's keep reading.

> Not giving up meeting together, as some are in the habit of doing, but encouraging one another—and all the more as you see the Day approaching. (Heb. 10:25)

This verse is so crucial. Each one of us has to do our part and hold on to the hope we profess. Then when we are weak, we need to be inspired by the love and good deeds of others. And then the author says do not give up meeting together, as some are in the habit of doing.

Now, we don't know why some got into the habit of not meeting together, but we can guess at it. For some it was just laziness. It's easier to stay in bed than to go to church. Once you get out of the habit of church, it's so easy to stay in the habit of not going back. Some may have gotten out of the habit because they had a bad experience. And I get that. People are messy. But…

Great relationships happen intentionally, not accidentally.

The church is not a product to consume; it's a family to belong to. The church is not a pastor or a denomination; it's people. The church is not a building; it's people building each other up for Jesus. Christians are the church, and we represent Jesus everywhere we go. If you are a Christian, what type of family member are you? Healthy family members contribute more than they consume. Going to a service is one part of the church. Church, however, is not attending a service. Church is people. Church is people hanging out and having fun in a way that honors God. Church is hospital visits. Church is showing up with food to support a family in need. Church is way more than an hour on Sunday morning. Church is not a building! It's people! Way too many Christians have given up meeting together because we "don't have time." We don't have time for small groups. We don't have time to volunteer at the church. We don't have time to build more relationships. We need to stop saying we don't have time. We need to be honest and say, "I'm not willing to make the time." Relationships are the conduit in which God uses to help us grow. You cannot love God and not love people. A relationship with God is a relationship with God's people. The two are connected.

I get all the reasons why we can't have community. I get that we are busy. I get how hard life can be. I get how messy people can be. Some people are straight up annoying. Some people are needy. Some people make me want to stay home and never come out to play. The only problem is I'm some people. Jerk! I frustrate myself. If I don't lead myself well, I ended up being selfish and ultimately harm myself. We can't live life alone. We weren't meant to, and we shouldn't try.

Let me be vulnerable with you. I have some wounds. I'm great at surface relationships. I have a lot of friends and people I stay connected with. But I have this insecurity that if someone gets too close to me they are not going to like what they see and they will leave.

That fear is then magnified by the fact that people that I care deeply about have actually left. It's difficult to find someone who will love you, warts and all. Part of this fear of people leaving is what drives me to be better. I read books, listen to podcasts, take personality profiles all with the hope of becoming better. But at times it's exhausting.

And at the heart of it is the question:

Am I worthy to be loved?

We wear masks to pretend to be better. We all have wounds from other people, and we all have a coping mechanism. We go to temporary pleasures like food, alcohol, sex, shopping, or even social media.

Social media is so addictive because there is an instant gratification of being liked. But this has led to even more shallow relationships. Simon Sinek is an amazing author and speaker, and he has spent a lot of time with millennials. He shares that following that I think applies to more than millennials, but it was said about them as a whole.

> Millennials will admit that many of their relationships are superficial, they will admit that they don't count on their friends, they don't rely on their friends. They have fun with their friends, but they also know that their friends will cancel on them when something better comes along. Deep meaningful relationships are not there because they never practiced the skill set and worse, they don't have the coping mechanisms to deal with stress. So when significant stress begins to show up in their lives, they're not turning to a person, they're turning to a device, they're turning to social media, they're turning to these things which offer temporary relief.

I don't think this is just millennials. Simon said, "Deep meaningful relationships are not there because they never practiced the skill set and worse, they don't have the coping mechanisms to deal with stress." I'm not sure very many of us have the coping mechanisms to deal with stress. And way too many of us have dealt with people leaving or hurting us, so the easy route is to disengage from real relationships and to turn to instant gratification.

So we have wounds, and the wounds lead us to retreat. It just becomes easier. Thankfully, Jesus does his best work through people's wounds.

The truth is that many people have a surface love for God, but until you allow Him to love your mess, you will always keep Him at arm's length.

You want to be loved, but do you truly believe God can love you? You see, in our minds we feel love is always earned. So it leads to the need to perform. If I perform, then people will love me. Some of you are so tired of performing, it has become easier to just push people away.

In America today, we have an epidemic of loneliness. We are wired for relationships, and when we don't have stable, life-giving relationships, it wreaks havoc on our bodies. Loneliness leads to anxiety and depression, and the effects of loneliness impact your body in negative ways.

Vivek Murthy, the surgeon general of the United States, has said many times in recent years that the most prevalent health issue in the country is not cancer or heart disease or obesity. It is isolation.

And a major problem with loneliness is that most of us don't think we are lonely. Loneliness seems like it is reserved for cat ladies or people who lack social skills. We think we aren't lonely because we have social media or because we have friends. But how often do you see people you would consider your best friend? One of my best friends lives in Georgia, and I see him two or three times a year. The couple that my wife and I say are our best friends has often said, "You guys are the best friends we have that we never see." I get all too well how busy life is. I get how inconvenient it can be to have healthy relationships. I'm a work in progress, but I'm trying to be intentional with my relationships.

Many people are lonely, but don't feel lonely. It's due to a newer social construct that came with cities, factories, and now even more with social media. It's called crowded isolation.

Crowded isolation: knowing lots of people but not having anyone truly know the real you.

Dr. Richard Schwartz is a Cambridge psychiatrist, and he has noted:

> When people with children become over scheduled, they don't shortchange their children, they shortchange their friendships. And the public health dangers of that are incredibly clear.

The public health dangers are severe. "In a meta-analysis of 3 million people, which controlled for confounding factors such as demographics and objective isolation, loneliness increased the odds of an early death by 26%." Think about that! If I found that I would have 26 percent more chance to win the lottery if I did one thing, I'd do it. If I win, I'd tithe 10 percent back to the church. Don't judge me. I don't play the lottery, but if I knew I had a high percentage to win I'd play. Don't get sidetracked. Stay on target. The point is not whether Christians should play the lottery. The point is that loneliness is literally killing us.

So what is the answer? We need scheduled time to invest in and be invested in. If we don't schedule it, we will prioritize the immediate needs.

Great relationships happen intentionally, not accidentally.

We need relationships.

In order to form healthy relationships, we have to prioritize them.

We love the idea of things happening naturally. We hate the thought of forcing authentic relationships. We don't want to manipulate or force relationships, so we resist scheduling relationships. The problem is, if we don't schedule it, they won't happen.

In order to figure out what we should prioritize, we need to figure out what we ultimately want in life. What is most important to us? As a Christian it should be based around the two things Jesus said were most important: loving God and loving people. We so often allow other things to dictate our schedule because we don't know what we value the most.

Death Is the Ultimate Expiration Date

Bonnie Ware is an Australian nurse who spent years caring for patients in the last twelve weeks of their life. When questioned about any regrets they had or anything they would do differently, she says, "Common themes surfaced again and again." Here are the top five themes that consistently came out of that question.

Top five regrets of the dying as witnessed by Bonnie Ware:

1. I wish I'd had the courage to live a life true to myself, not the life others expected of me.
2. I wish I hadn't worked so much.
3. I wish I'd had the courage to express my feelings.
4. I wish I had stayed in touch with my friends.
5. I wish that I had let myself be happier.

You want to know what's absent from that list? Jerk-like behaviors. The jerk gets in the way of healthy relationships. I don't know anyone who likes to think about death. In fact, most people like to not think about death. But death is one of those few things that makes us reflect on the life we are living. Death is the great expiration date. It's the great deadline that we all face. If the jerk is winning in your life, then think about the legacy he will leave when you die. We think we will have time to make up for our jerk-like behaviors, but what if we don't? I thought number 2 and 4 were particularly interesting. I wonder if working so much is a regret for those who are dying because it took them away from those they love the most. I doubt they have a regret from having a job. I wonder if they simply regret allowing the job to dictate so much of their life. Number 4 is interesting because it's exactly what this chapter is about. Many people do not stay in contact with friends because it's not easy. Life gets in the way. Remember those friends I mentioned that said me and my wife are the best friends they never see? One way I've tried to fix that is by being in a small group with them through the church. If life gets crazy busy, we still know we will see them at least once a week.

A Story about Friendship and Free Dessert

For a few years I was a part of an amazing community through CrossFit gym. I didn't know going in that I would form great friendships through this gym. One of the reasons the friendships started is because we saw each other on a consistent basis. Two of the guys, Nick and Kris, worked out on Friday mornings. Because Friday is my day off, I would schedule my workout during the time they were at the gym. We would often talk for good amounts of time after the workout was complete. Unfortunately, our gym closed and with that we stopped seeing each other as much. We all went to the same church, but there is limited time to hang out. Their schedules didn't permit them to be a part of the small group

I led, so we became friends who never saw one another. One day after church one of the guys suggest we go to lunch. He even called it his small group. It took some time and schedule juggling, but we were able to find a lunch time that worked for all of us. What happened next has been an unexpected but amazing part of the story.

The first week we met I don't think any of us had expectations. We simply wanted to catch up and prioritize spending time together. We ordered our food and then went to get our drinks as we waited for it to be ready. By the time we got our drinks, they called our names to let us know the food was ready. It seemed really quick to us, but when we walked up to the counter, the manager said, "I'm so sorry, you guys had to wait so long. Dessert is on me today." When we got to our table the three of us joked that it did not take long to get our food, but we are very thankful for free dessert. At the end we pulled out the calendars on our phones to pick our date for the next month. The next month rolls around, and we go to the same place.

For the second month it actually took longer to get our food, and they didn't offer free dessert. No worries. We weren't mad. We did laugh at how we got free dessert at our first meeting for having to wait so long (a minute) for our food. On the second meeting we laughed, shared stories, and ate barbeque. At Mission BBQ, they send around the staff to ask if you need anything aka the Chick-fil-A way. When they came to our table, a nice woman named Amanda asked if she could get us anything. Me being the full-of-dad-jokes guy that I am said, "Not unless you are giving out free dessert." I expected her to give me a courteous chuckle, but she quickly replied, "Are you military?" My friend Nick spoke up and said, "No, but this is our pastor and we are meeting for our small group." Amanda smiled but never promised anything.

We all chuckled, and then she went to another table. It was at that moment that I hit myself for missing an opportunity to drop some pastor humor. When she asked if we were in the military, I should have joked, "Yes, ma'am! I'm in the Lord's Army. Does that count for free dessert?" Okay, that's bad. I'm glad I didn't say that. I digress.

After a few moments Amanda comes back to our table with some amazing peach cobbler. And it was on the house! Score. That's two months in a row of free dessert. At this luncheon the guys and I set up our next time to meet. The following month we showed back up to Mission BBQ. We had zero expectations for free dessert but were all very interested in seeing if we could keep the streak alive. For our third meeting Amanda was working again. While we were eating, she brought dessert out to us. It was glorious. We are in there like swimwear. From this moment on we are confident the streak will continue. That is, until the next month.

On our fourth meeting we showed up and Amanda wasn't working. When we didn't see her, we asked the employee at the cash register. She said it was her day off, but then asked why we were inquiring about Amanda. One of the guys quickly mentioned how we meet at Mission BBQ every month for our small group and Amanda gives us free dessert. The employee behind the cash register said, "Oh, I can do that for you guys this month!" Score! We go to get our drinks and then they call our name for our food. There is no dessert, but we are used to Amanda bringing it out to us later on. We go to sit down with lots of hope and anticipation. This month's lunch was full of laughs, inside jokes, and some real moments about fatherhood and life. We get finished, and there is no dessert. Kris comes up with an idea that he will go up to order the desserts, and best case it will jog cash register girl's memory. Worst case he'll buy the dessert and the streak will end. No big deal. When he walks up to the cash register employee, she says, "Have they not brought your dessert out to you yet?" Kris told her they had not and offered to pay for the dessert. She quickly got some dessert for us and rejected his attempt to pay.

On month five the streak was really alive, and Amanda was working. Free dessert once again. On month six Amanda was not working. One of the guys tried dropping a hint to the cash register employee, but it went nowhere. During our lunch we all concluded that the streak was over. At that moment an employee named Sabrina approached our table. She was a new employee and did work for their guest relations. We mentioned that we were meeting for our monthly church small group, and she asked what church we went to. I asked if she went to church, and wouldn't you know it, she went to church with one of my pastor friends. She ended up sharing her story and then...you guessed it...she brought us free dessert. She also had us sign up for their VIP members club. That gave us a coupon for a free dessert! The next month we missed Amanda but used our coupon. The streak lives on.

For month eight we saw Amanda and let her know that we missed seeing her. She told us to contact her ahead of time so she could make sure she was on the schedule. We now are on the calendar for free dessert at Mission BBQ. We've continued to meet at Mission BBQ once a month. We've invited staff to attend church, gotten to know some cool people, and deepened our relationships with each other. Why do I tell you all of this? It's because great things happen when you are intentional.

I'm a better person because of my monthly lunch meetings. I wish we had time to hang out more than once a month. Maybe one day we will. But for now, all three of us are experiencing life change and a lot of free dessert. Since those first few months, we have added doing a Bible study together through the app YouVersion. I see real spiritual growth in the guys! It's always a highlight of my week when we meet! Great relationships happen intentionally, not accidentally.

Entitlement and Friendship

I mentioned this earlier, but I understand the rub against being intentional with relationships. It feels like it's not authentic if we have to plan it. I'd like to offer another way of looking at it. To not be intentional with relationships is a form of entitlement. Entitlement is the feeling of having a right to something. We aren't entitled to great relationships. They don't just happen. Great marriages don't just happen. Great friendships rarely just happen. Great relationships with neighbors and coworkers don't happen accidentally. It's a form of entitlement to expect great relationships without putting forth great effort. Way too often we want uphill results while putting in downhill effort. I'm convinced that if I wasn't intentional, I'd never see my friends. My friend Dan and I scheduled walking trails together. My friend Jamey and I scheduled a book club so we could hang out and learn at the same time. My friend Rob and I scheduled a monthly lunch. My best friend from college, Blake, and I scheduled regular calls. He doesn't have social media, so if we are not intentional, we don't connect. My buddy Andrew does a great job of reaching out when a new movie comes out. After writing that, I realize it doesn't sound very manly. I'm going to intentionally work on connecting with some of my friends over eating beef jerky, watching pro football, and spitting.

Relationships by nature are difficult. It's not easy to have a relationship with anyone. Everybody is selfish, jacked up, and comes with baggage. You are included in this everyone. At the same time there are some amazing people out there. There are also some people who have potential to be amazing if someone would love them like Jesus. At the end of your life, what will you care about the most? I'm betting it will be relationships.

I want to take you through an exercise that should help you figure out what direction should you be aiming at in life. This is going to help you figure out what's ultimately important to you. This is going to help us number our days. When you realize what is most important to you, you'll find that you don't have time to be a jerk. In order to do this I need you to get out something to write with. A lot of people will skip over this, but I encourage you not to. What do you have to lose? Are you ready? Here we go.

In a moment I'm going to invite you to close your eyes. In order for this to work you need to eliminate all distractions. Silence your phone. Be still. Get quiet. When you are ready close your eyes, I want to picture something. At first this may seem strange, but stick with me on this. I want you to picture a casket. This is your casket. I want you to try and imagine your funeral. Imagine who is there. Imagine the smell of the flowers. Imagine who is speaking. What stories are going to be shared? Imagine what you want said. Are you there? If you are still reading this, your eyes aren't closed. No matter, you can close them after you read this next sentence. What legacy did you leave with the people that attended your funeral? The people that are closest to you, how are they feeling? Is there a sadness with a heaviness or a sadness with a tinge of joy because of how you lived your life? Can you see it?

Now take a moment to answer these questions.

- Who are the most important people at your funeral?
- If you died today, what would people say about you?
- What do you want them to say?
- Does how you live match what you want to be said?
- Who do you wish you spent more time with?

Teach us to number our days, that we may gain a heart of wisdom. (Ps. 90:12)

Number your days. This season you are currently in is a short season in your life. Make the most of it. If you are in high school you get to choose how your high school career goes. You can put off living for God until you are older, or you can decide "Right now, I'm going to live for God." If you are single, then you can decide now, "My single years are a gift from God." That is, you can do things now that you will not be able to do when you get married. Don't waste your single years. Don't waste your single years practicing bad behaviors. Practice now being a person of integrity. If you are married, you can choose right now, "I'm going to have a marriage that honors God." Don't waste this season. If you are seventy years old, don't waste this season! Your days are not over. You are not dead. No matter what season you are in start making the most of it today. Make the most of this season by intentionally investing in people. I wear a T-shirt that says, "Live a type of life that the preacher doesn't have to lie at your funeral." That's what we are going for with this exercise. Whatever you wrote in the blanks provided now serves as your guide. Become intentional.

We all need deadlines because we procrastinate. Here's your deadline. Start today. Trying to cram a life well lived in the last days of your life just doesn't work.

> Improvement doesn't happen in a day,
> but it must be daily. (John Maxwell)

You might feel overwhelmed with the items in that exercise. You might not know where to start. Start by taking one intentional step in that direction. Then take another. Do those steps consistently, and you'll be headed in the right direction. Here are some examples of making intentional friendships:

- Set up a regular time to meet. A small group, coffee meeting, lunch or dinner, monthly hangout, etc. The key is to intentionally plan something and do that thing on a regular basis.
- Use social media. Instead of being passive become active. Support the people in your life on social media. Be intentional by creating a reminder in your phone to encourage the people you love on social media.

- Use drive time to connect. My wife, Monica, uses an app called Marco Polo to connect with other women. Whenever she has time in the car, she turns off the music and starts intentionally reaching out. She connects with over forty women using this app. It takes time, but it's so worth it. At the end of your life you probably won't remember very many car rides. What if we used this time to be intentional?
- When you think something nice, say it. This world is negative! It's like what Truett Cathy once said, "How do you know if someone needs encouragement? If they are breathing." Committing to say something nice whenever you think it is, is an intentional way to build into other people.
- Prioritize family meals. Turn off the TV and put away smartphones. Eating together has great potential for people to connect.
- Become a connector of people. You can only connect to so many people. When you meet someone who needs to be connected, invite them to a hangout where you introduce them to someone you think they will connect with. That's intentional.
- Use the app YouVersion to do a Bible study with some friends. It's awesome! You can discuss the Bible study and stay connected from your phone.
- When you think about someone, reach out. A quick text or message goes a long way.
- Schedule time to connect. Often, if I do not put it in my calendar, I will not remember to do it. Put a reminder in your phone to call, text, or reach out to someone you care about. It feels forced at first, but eventually it becomes natural.

- Whether it's once a week, month, or even every few months, the key is to intentionally carve out time to connect. With social media it's become that much easier. I know it's some effort to be the person who plans things. Just remember that great relationships don't happen accidentally, they happen intentionally.

Win for this chapter: Make plan for your intentional investment. Who is it going to be with? What are you going to do?

Questions for Further Reflection

1. Who is your closest friend? How often do you see them?
2. What characteristics does a great friend have?
3. How many of the characteristics you just thought of do you have?
4. Would you say you are lonely? Why or why not?
5. If you want to have great friends, you must be a great friend. On a scale of 1 to 10 (1 being awful and 10 being awesome), how would you rank yourself as a friend?
6. What would it take for you to move up to a higher number?

CHAPTER 14

Submit Is Not a Four-Letter Word

As discussed throughout this book we all have a set of rules and expectations in which we live by. They are often difficult to name because they are so ingrained in us. You can start to tell what rules you live by when you examine what you give a stank face to.

Stank face—the look you naturally give to someone when they have offended you. Typically involves a glare or a reaction similar to smelling something really bad.

Now there are versions of the stank face:

There is the side eye where you make a stank face and look at someone with your side eyes.

There's the literal disgust stank face. That is, you are disgusted by what you just saw or heard.

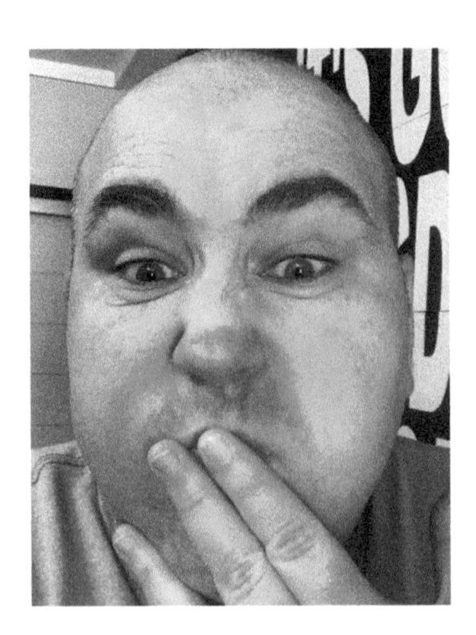

Then there's the wide-eyed stank face.

You have a stank face. When you get offended by someone else, you naturally make a face. If you don't, it's because you have a poker face but inside your mind you are making a stank face.

There are certain things that are so ingrained in you that you do them without even thinking. If you could put it in words, you would say, "This is just how I do things." The problem is that every human you meet has spent their life playing by the rules they have learned. Oftentimes, those rules do not match the rules you learned to play. So often the deepest hurts, frustrations, resentments, and fights come from someone intentionally or unintentionally breaking one of our rules. In relationships we know people cannot read our minds, but we often treat them like they can. Humans have a few basic needs, but often it is difficult to put to words what we are feelings. It's why at times our faces communicate what we are feeling.

Humans are simple creatures with complex emotions.

We are simple in that we only need a few things to survive. Give me air to breathe, some food, a place to sleep, and companionship; and I'm good to go. There are a few basic necessities for humans. Our emotions on the other hand are difficult to figure out. They may feel like simple emotions, but discovering the root behind the emotions is complex. Often a stank face is given, and when asked for an explanation, it's difficult to give.

I'm convinced that the vast majority of our relational issues come from miscommunication and mismanaging our emotions. Because our emotions are so strong, the natural response is to try to control things. When we feel out of control, we try to control others. The truth is you cannot control anyone. If you haven't picked up on that so far, then please commit to reread this book. It's been a major theme.

Jesus said that greatest commandment is to love God with all your heart and to love others. Because of this, Christians should have the healthiest relationships. We should have the healthiest marriages. We should have the healthiest friendships. We should have the healthiest work environments. Even when Christians have conflict it should be an example to others. Christians aren't exempt from conflict. With some practice and the grace of God, we should become examples to others in how to have healthy conflicts that reflect Jesus.

I truly hope you are putting into practice what you have learned from this book. Just know that this chapter deals with one of the last obstacle in killing the jerk. It's a doozy of a chapter. I'm convinced that this chapter holds the key to finally killing the inner jerk. When this chapter is applied by both people in a relationship, I believe a healthy relationship will result.

In the early church the apostle Paul gave some instructions for relationships. Paul is a prime-time player in Scripture. He wrote over half of the New Testament. Paul gives a very controversial scripture. It's not as controversial as it first appears, but just know that some of you will want to push back on what he says when you first see it. Stick around. Please don't stop reading this book or throw it across the room or get on Amazon and write a negative review. As you read this and you are tempted to write a negative review, please remember two things: (1) Remember the name of this book is *Boundaries* by Henry Cloud. (2) Remember the twenty-four-hour rule. I kid, I kid. I hope you know me enough now to give me the benefit of the doubt. I hope that you will read this chapter with an open mind. I hope you'll not read your own context into this chapter. Read this chapter with an open mind and look at what the information says, not what you want it to say. Seriously though, don't make a judgment until you've read the entire chapter. Are you ready? Here is the verse:

> Submit to one another out of reverence
> for Christ. (Eph. 5:21)

The verse we just read starts off with the word *submit*. That's an awful word because of our modern-day context. When I think of *submit*, I think of old school rastling. Not wrestling. Rastling. I'm talking about Ricky the Dragon Steamboat. I'm talking about Roddy Rider Piper. I'm talking about the Macho Man Randy Savage. I'm talking about Rick Whoooo Flair. The thirteen-time heavyweight champion of the world. To be the man you've got to beat the man. The limousine-riding, jet-flying, kiss-stealing, wheeling-and-dealing, mean son of gun. Whooo! Now some of you know exactly what I'm talking about. You are smelling what the Rob is cooking. Others of you don't have a fat clue what is happening right now. That's okay. I promise you'll get it soon.

Whether you like rastling or not, you need to know that all the good rastlers have finishing moves. Some of the best professional wrestlers finishing moves are a submission move. That is, they force the other person to submit by tapping out. Rick Flair has the famous figure-four leg lock. That is a submission move. It's been said that it's impossible to break. It's forcing ones will on another person.

When we hear the word *submit*, it can be easy to think of someone forcing another person to give up. That sounds horrible. In fact, this verse has been used by some to exert power over others. I don't think that's what the Scripture had in mind. You'll see this in a few moments.

When Scripture uses the word *submit*, we read our context into it. We read a 1950s style of husband-and-wife relationship where the husband rules the roost and tells the wife what to do. We think of an environment where children are seen but not heard. We think of a place where one person has the power and gets to do what they want while everyone else takes on the form of Dobby the house elf. If that references misses you, then think of a servant who has no say in what they do. The idea of being forced to submit is horrible, and it makes sense why many buck at the word. I want to show you how that's not the case when Scripture uses the word *submit*. The scriptural understanding of submission:

Submit—voluntary yielding to someone else.

Have you ever been in traffic and one lane had to merge with the other? And there seems to always be that one person who refuses to yield. They just power their way into the lane. I'm not talking about the accidental or unintentional lane merger. I'm talking about the person who knows the lane is coming to an end but puts their needs in front of everyone else's. That person is acting like a jerk. Often we honk our horns at people who cut us off or force their way into a lane. Some of us even give the universal symbol for bad drivers. It's a lot like we are number 1. On the other hand, have you ever needed someone to let you into the other lane? When someone doesn't have to but voluntarily yields so that you can change lanes, it's amazing. I wish there was a version of a car horn that would say thank you for moments like that. I'd love to tap my horn, and it says, "Thank you." I've been in situations where either because I wasn't paying attention or I simply wasn't aware I needed someone else to let me in. When someone volunteers to let me in, I celebrate them. They are a hero! This is the idea of submission.

Submission does not mean obey. In fact, the word *obedience* is never mentioned in Scripture when it comes to wives and husbands. I don't think we are to obey friends or others that we have relationships with. Obedience is not submission. Look at what the Scripture says:

> Submit to one another. (Eph. 5:21)

Submitting takes two. Why? Because it takes two to make a thing go right. It takes two to make it out of sight. Submitting is not forcing anyone to do anything. Submitting is when, for the good of the relationship, you put the other person first. It's a choice you make for yourself, not for someone else. I choose to submit when I put my wife first. I choose to submit when I put my friends first. I don't submit out of guilt or compulsion but out of love. I believe good parents understand this. I could care less about Pokemon, Paw Patrol, or JoJo Siwa. I learned about them all because I submitted to my kids. When my kids are interested in something, I try my best to find interest in it because I'm interested in them. Submission doesn't mean my kids are in charge. I don't obey my kids. As the parent I'm still in charge. My wife and I set their bedtime, discipline, and values. Because I care about someone, I lean in by putting them first. This insight was even more heightened to me when I learned the opposite of submit.

The Opposite of Submission

The opposite of submit is disagreement.

I don't know if that surprises you, but I was caught off guard by that. It makes sense though. In a relationship when you have a disagreement it causes a rift in the relationship. When we disagree with someone, it causes us to feel frustrated. What do we do when we disagree? We try to argue, we fight, or we punish someone when we disagree with them. I hope the chapters I've written will help many handle disagreements in a healthy way. It's not easy, and the reason it's not easy is because we do not like to submit. We would rather argue, fight, or break off a relationship, then find a way to submit.

Let me ask you a question. Have you ever changed your opinion because someone argued with you? I have had my opinion changed in a conversation, but rarely have I wanted to change my thinking because someone was arguing with me. If anything, I want to dig my heels in and argue in support of my view more when someone wants to argue. In the history of social media, has anyone changed their opinion because of an argument? The more someone disagrees with us, the harder we push back. It's been said famously that the definition of insanity is if you do the same thing over and over again and expect different results. When we apply this to how we fight in relationships, we all should be locked away in an asylum. When the inner jerk comes out, he never thinks about if he is being effective. All he thinks about is winning the argument or fights. Jerk.

Now the question is how does a typical disagreement end? Typically, a disagreement ends with one person walking away or one person trying to control the other person. When someone walks away, it's not submission. It's avoidance. When someone doesn't run away, they will try force the other person to submit. We do this by trying to control them. There are a few ways we try to force others to submit to us by controlling them.

Ways We Try to Control Others:

1. Fear—threats, punishment, yelling
2. Withholding—intimacy, silent treatment, isolation
3. Gifts with a cost—done to get something in return, are used as debt to repay
4. Guilt—manipulation, making people feel bad in order to get what we want
5. Sarcasm/insults—trying to change people to be what you want them to be

That is not an exhaustive list. It is a list of the common ones I see. When someone disagrees with us, we fight back.

When we fight, we try to become bigger than the other person in a way that scares them into submission. We are trying to force them to submit. When we disagree and it leads to yelling, we are trying to scare them into submission. When we use guilt, it is an unhealthy way to try to cause someone to submit. Healthy relationships are not based on force. Healthy relationships don't try to control one another. Healthy relationships understand that in order to win both people must compromise. That's mutual submission. Submission is something you give, not something you force. Controlling others is dangerous. In fact, that's the big idea for this chapter.

Big Idea: Submission is something you give, not something you force.

Christians are called to submit to one another, not control one another. Now remember submission is not obedience. Biblical submission is not having one person in power and the other doing whatever they say. My son told me the other day that he couldn't wait to grow up. When I said why, he said, "So I can do whatever I want." Good luck with that, Bucko. As an adult I'm not always in charge. There are times where I have to choose to submit because of someone's position of authority. When I see an ambulance's lights flashing in my rearview mirror, I choose to submit. I don't have to. I could refuse, and there would be a consequence to that, but it's still a choice. When I wasn't the boss, I submitted to the standards of the job. I came in when I was told. I didn't have to. I had a choice. If I refused to submit, I would get fired but I still had a choice. These are examples of one-sided submission. I don't ask the ambulance to submit to me. I didn't expect my bosses to submit to me. When it comes to personal relationships (friendships, marriage, etc.), the position of authority shouldn't matter.

Submission is not a tug-a-war where one person wins and one person loses. Submission in relationships isn't about having a title or position of authority. Submission is not a tug-a-war, rastling, or MMA fighting. The best example of biblical submission is a three-legged race. Did you ever do a three-legged races? In some ways they are horrible. I can get everywhere faster not being attached to someone else. When you are in a three-legged race, the only way to win is to submit to the other person. It doesn't matter if you are faster, male or female, Republican or Democrat, like Coke or Pepsi, if you want to win a three-legged race, you have to submit. In order to win the race, each person has to commit to the other person that for the good of the team I will put you first. You have to run in sync, and in order to do that you have to agree on what being *in sync* means. To some it means a boy band from the nineties that was superior to the Backstreet Boys. If you don't like boy bands from the 90s, then bye bye bye. To the rest of us being in sync means we agree upon a few standards, rules, and expectations; and we do our part to keep them. When one person tries to do their own thing, both people are hurt. When one person demands to have their way, calamity ensues.

As a student pastor I once witnessed this. One of our student leaders ran a three-legged race with one of the junior high students. They weren't equals by any means. This student leader was one of our more athletic, taller, and more competitive leaders. When they ran the race, they jumped out to a quick lead because of the brute strength of the student leader. We all laughed because the student wasn't doing anything to help win the race. He essentially jumped on for the ride. Pretty quickly the student leader was slowed down by having a student attached to himself. The student was being dragged down the field by the leader. It worked for a little bit, but eventually, it became difficult and both ended up falling to the ground. Isn't that true in relationships? When one person is selfish, doesn't it impact multiple people? Christians are not called to control people; we are called to submit. Some people stink at relationships because it's always about them. Being all about you is not a relationship, it's a dictatorship. It may help you feel in control, but it's miserable for others. When we disagree, we are tempted to try to figure out a way to control the other person in order to get what we want. The problem is, when we try to control others, we are communicating that we matter and they don't.

Control says, "I matter, and you don't."
Mutual submission says, "You matter, and so do I."

You see, submission isn't about not getting what you want. It's about compromising so both people gets what they ultimately want. Nothing reveals immaturity like not getting our way. Mature relationships are built on compromise. Our differences divide, but when we compromise, we build a bridge toward each other. Ultimately, if I want a happy marriage, I have to make some compromises and at the same time so does my wife. That's mutual submission. It's the same with friendship, coworkers, and neighbors. If I want to have healthy relationships, I need to make the choice to submit. If both people submit to each other, then the ultimate goal is winning the race. Whenever there is relational discord, it is because one or both people are unwilling to submit.

We fight for what we want, and then even if we win, we lose. We lose because we damage the relationship. In almost every situation there is a compromise. Being unwilling to compromise is a lack of submission. I think one of the reasons many people fear submission is because we think we won't get what we want if we submit. First off all, think about how selfish that is. Second of all, if you get what you want but you lose a relationship, you still lose. There is almost always a compromise.

My wife likes when I plan a date. She doesn't like when we go back and forth with, "What do you want to do?" "I don't care, what do you want to do?" Early in our relationship I tried to take the initiative to plan a date. When Monica didn't like the date idea or wanted something different, I took it as a form of rejection. My natural reaction was to not plan dates. That's not a compromise, and that's not submission. After I got over myself, I brainstormed a better way to do date night. Monica ultimately wanted to see that I put in initiative, but at the same time she does like having a say. She just doesn't want to be the one that makes the decision. So my compromise was, whenever I plan a date, I come up with three potential options. I present the options, and she gets to choose from the three. It shows that I took some initiative, and it protects my sensitive ego from feeling rejected. Win, win. I believe that for almost every situation there is a compromise. Being unwilling to compromise is a selfish way to try and control a situation or person.

Moving On

Please note that submission should never be mistaken for abuse. If someone is using their power to hurt you physically or emotionally, then please leave. I believe most people reading this chapter will get that, but I want to make sure it's clear. Abuse is a form of control. It's unhealthy. That's not submission, and it is 100 percent not what God is talking about.

Submission is knowing my strengths and weaknesses. Where I am weak, I need you to be strong. Where you are weak, I will be strong. It doesn't matter who has the authority if everyone is miserable. If you have the authority but you don't have healthy relationships, what have you won? With control, it's my way or the highway. You better like what I like, agree with what I agree with, clean like I clean; or I'll make you pay. With mutual submission it's about finding a compromise so everyone wins. Submission is not about controlling others; it's about controlling yourself. You get to choose to submit. Think about how much joy it brings you when someone lets you cut in front of them in traffic. You get to create that same type of joy when you choose to put others first.

Now this can be tough teaching for us. The idea of submission is taught multiple times in Scripture. Other than having healthy relationships, is there another reason this idea is taught? Let's see how Paul ends the verse. It's ultimately the reason why Christians are called to submit.

> Submit to one another out of reverence for Christ. (Eph. 5:21)

Why are Christians called to submit? Out of reverence for Christ. This is so powerful! Jesus is God in the flesh. The most powerful being in the universe submitted. Not because he had too, but because he wanted to. Jesus didn't feel like dying on a cross for us. He submitted for our good. Jesus didn't feel like being tortured for our good. He submitted for our good. For our good Jesus laid down His own rights. Jesus didn't have to die. He chose to die. Scripture teaches that sin needed a payment and Jesus paid that payment with His life. For you to experience a spiritual connection with God, Jesus submitted for you and for me. Look at what Scripture says:

> Therefore if you have any encouragement from being united with Christ, if any comfort from his love, if any common sharing in the Spirit, if any tenderness and compassion, then make my joy complete by being like-minded, having the same love, being one in spirit and of one mind. Do nothing out of selfish ambition or vain conceit. Rather, in humility value others above yourselves, not looking to your own interests but each of you to the interests of the others. In your relationships with one another, have the same mindset as Christ Jesus: Who, being in very nature God, did not consider equality with God something to be used to his own advantage; rather, he made himself nothing by taking the very nature of a servant, being made in human likeness. (Phil. 2:1–7)

Okay, I know that was a lot of scripture. Did you read it? Don't skim it. It's foundational for Christians. We are to put others first (submission) because that's what Jesus did for us. When we do this, we move as one. If you watch almost any team sport that wins a championship, one of the players will say something to the degree of, "Everyone played as one." There is a player who gets the MVP and other players who get more attention, but in order to win it takes each player doing their part and submitting to the others. In the moment the inner jerk will say, "Fight for what's yours!" At the end of the day, if everyone is fighting to have their own personal victories, no one wins. We all win when we mutually submit to one another.

I don't feel like playing outside with my kids. I hate the outdoors. I'm what you'd call indorsey. Everyone is always trying to force the outdoors on me like it doesn't come with the potential to do me great harm. If the outdoors is so great, why do we need sunscreen in the summer, bug spray, umbrellas, coats etc.? It's like the outdoors is constantly trying to kill us, and the only way to enjoy it is to slap on chemicals and various tactical gear to survive the elements. No, thank you! When I go inside, I don't have to spray on bug spray or sunscreen. I don't have to worry about an umbrella. When I am hot, I can control the thermostat. We cannot control other people, but I sure can control the thermostat. Don't even get me started on camping. I don't have enough vacation days to pretend to be homeless. I digress. Point being, I don't feel like playing with my kids outdoors, but I submit to them. When they want to play outside and I'm available, I go.

My friend sent me a podcast the other day. I know he loves podcasts. I knew he wouldn't send it to me if he didn't think I would like it. I don't love podcasts. I had no desire to listen to this podcast. I listened because I submitted to my friend. And guess what? I loved the podcast. It was very enjoyable and beneficial.

My wife doesn't give a rip about basketball. When the Lakers were in the finals in 2010, she stayed well past midnight watching the games with me. Not only that but she memorized the starting lineup, wore a jersey, and made all my favorite snacks for me to watch the game. She did this partly because I cannot stay up past 10:00 p.m. unless I'm eating. She doesn't give a rip about basketball, but she submitted. I didn't ask her to. She chose to on her own.

These examples are supposed to point the way to the benefits of mutual submission. When we mutually submit, we end up with harmony in the relationship. Sure it involves some compromise, but in the long run it's much more enjoyable. If you get what you want but no one goes with you, it's a loss.

If you have a problem with mutual submission, change your understanding of submission. Submission is not a manner of weakness. It's a matter of strength. A strong person can willingly submit for the good of the relationship. See Jesus for this example. You don't make people to submit, you choose to submit.

This chapter's Win: Ask a friend or family member, "In what area do you see me trying to control our relationship?"

Questions for Further Reflection

1. Before reading this chapter, how would you have defined submission?
2. What is a current problem you see? How could submission help solve this problem?
3. What are some ways you try to control others?
4. How can you let go of some of that control?
5. What does it look like to submit to Jesus? When we get this right, it makes it a lot easier to submit to others.

CHAPTER 15

You Are Not a Jerk

Identity is incredibly powerful. Until we know who we are, we will struggle with what to do. Until we know who we are, we will struggle with responding instead of reacting to conflict. Until we know who we are, we will continue to have a blind eye to the inner jerk.

> In the egoic state, your sense of self, your identity, is derived from your thinking mind—in other words, what your mind tells you about yourself: the storyline of you, the memories, the expectations, all the thoughts that go through your head continuously and the emotions that reflect those thoughts. All those things make up your sense of self. (Eckhart Tolle)

This is an important thing to discover. It's not a one-time discovery. It's a lifelong pursuit. To help you discover your identity, it's important to answer one question.

Who Are You?

Men and women tend to form their identity differently. When it comes to men, we typically form our identity based on what we do. This is why guys often lead with what they do for a job. If a guy feels insecure about his job, he may quickly go to his hobbies or something else he is proud of doing.

Women on the other hand typically tend to find their identity in who they know. This is why often a married women might lead with, "I'm married to _____" or "These are my kids." For some, it might be their friends, social group, or parents. No matter if you are male or female or if you can relate to those generalizations or not, the key thing to know about identity is...

Identity is ultimately formed in relationship to something else.

This is crucial in understanding who we are. We tend to form our identity in someone or something else. So let me ask you, who are you? There are typically four ways people answer that question.

Four ways people answer "Who I am?" are the following:

1. My job
2. My talents or hobbies
3. Who I know
4. I don't know

You don't have to be a Christian to try and find your identity. Many find their identity in their job, hobbies, or who they know. Remember, we form our identity in relationship to something else. There are lots of studies and books on identity, but here is what I've found to be true. When you find your identity in anything other than God, when that thing goes away, you lose who you are. For example, if you find your identity in your job, what happens if you lose that job? Or if you find your identity in being a parent, what happens when your kids grow up and move out? If you find your identity in another person, what happens if they move away or change their relationship to you? If you find your identity in your talents, then what happens when you can no longer do that thing that you are good at? Even more likely, what do you do when someone does what you do better than you? When we don't know who we are, we see others as competition. We are constantly sizing up others to see if we have worth. This works in our favor as long as we are better than others, but what happens when someone better comes along? Instead of celebrating them, we will compete.

I make a locally famous-for-people-who-know-me chocolate chip cookie. It's how I raised the money to publish this book. Years ago, I got a recipe from one of my wife's fourth grade students. I've used it for years, and it has become a thing I'm known for. When someone is sad or sick, I bring them cookies. When we have company over for dinner, I make cookies. When it's national chocolate chip cookie day, I make cookies. We often make cookie drops for our friends. Whenever people eat them, they act like they've tasted heaven. I didn't choose the cookie life, the cookie life chose me. My friend Chris started making chocolate chip cookies, and he was strategically trying to win people over. Our friend Wes moved to a new house and Chris brought him and his family cookies. I immediately get a text from Wes telling me how amazing Chris's cookies are and that they are better than mine. I didn't know that making chocolate chip cookies was a part of my identity until I got that text. Let me tell you that in that moment, I didn't celebrate. I wasn't excited about this news. I was thinking, *Cookies are my thing. Go get your own thing, Judas...I mean, Chris.*

I then talked to my wife and said, "We need to find a way to get over to Wes's house." So a few days later, my wife, Monica, and I went over to Wes's house and you know we brought cookies.

We are sitting around eating them and without asking, Wes's daughter, Audrey, said, "This cookie is way better than Mr. Chris's."

I immediately pulled out the camera on my phone and said, "Can you say that again?"

How petty is that? Jerk! My point is when you find your identity in what you do, it starts to crumble when someone can do what you do better. You view life as a competition. We stop seeing people as having worth, and we start to view them as competition. It's difficult to love people we are competing with. The inner jerk doesn't want to celebrate with others who threaten their identity. I see this often in church circles. Churches act like competitors instead of being on the same team. I see this with people. People criticize others when they don't know who they are. In some crazy way, tearing down others makes us feel better about ourselves. Jerks!

This is why I think finding our identity in Jesus is so crucial. Jesus doesn't change. Jesus doesn't leave us. When everything else crumbles around us Jesus is a constant. Your job may change, but Jesus doesn't. Your skills may erode, but Jesus doesn't. A loved one may leave you, but Jesus doesn't. So the question is how do we find our identity in Jesus? In order to get to our identity we need to look at a foundation for our identity. We are going to look at this in the Apostle Paul's letter called Ephesians.

> As for you, you were dead in your transgressions and sins, in which you used to live when you followed the ways of this world and of the ruler of the kingdom of the air, the spirit who is now at work in those who are disobedient. (Eph. 2:1–2)

There is a way that seems right, but it's not of God. It's the way of the jerk! Paul says that the natural way that we think leads to sin and death. No one has to teach us how to be selfish. No one has to teach us how to be insecure. No one has to teach us how to shame others. It's natural. This natural, unhealthy, way of thinking is what Paul refers to as the "way of this world." It's natural and common, but it is so destructive. Remember your identity is ultimately in relationship to something else. So who you follow matters. Your identity is in relationship to something else. This is why it's so crucial to have your identity formed in something healthy and unchanging. When we are disobedient to God, we know we are not following God. When we don't want to obey God, we know we are not following God. Whenever we don't want to love God, love people, or make a difference, we know we aren't following God.

Following God is a choice you make. It's like my friend John says, "You are only as close to God as you want to be. How close are you?" This is a theme in multiple letters Paul wrote. He often wrote about how in Jesus we are new creations. That is we are to think and react differently than those without God. We aren't perfect, but we should be working on becoming the best versions of ourselves. Look at what Paul says in Romans 12:2.

> Do not conform to the pattern of this world, but be transformed by the renewing of your mind. Then you will be able to test and approve what God's will is—his good, pleasing and perfect will. (Rom. 12:2)

Do not conform to the pattern of this world, but be transformed. That's an intentional choice. How do we follow God, we have to renew our mind. That's intentional. God is the power source for change. We can't force God to move, but you better believe we have to do everything we can to show up ready for him to change us. People don't ruin their lives accidentally. They ruin them on decision at a time. People don't change their lives accidentally. They do so by making one positive change at a time.

Negative voices in our head have to be fought against. Don't just accept them. If you are feeling less, then it's an identity issue. When we are feeling insecure, it's an identity issue. If you are feeling like a jerk, it's an identity issue. The good news is that you are not alone in this struggle against negativity.

Studies show we talk to ourselves fifty thousand times a day. And studies have found that, on average, 80 percent of self-talk is negative.

What you believe about yourself is your truth. That's your identity. These negative thoughts when they come don't go away easily. It's a fight. Jerk! So often we are so self-deceived that we believe we are too broken to be fixed. I love the quote by John Milton…

> The mind is its own place, and in itself, can make a heaven out of hell, a hell of heaven. (John Milton)

What if your circumstances aren't as bad as you think they are? What if your life isn't as bad as you think it is? What if it's not a matter of having blessings as it is having a positive identity? This is why identity is so important. When you don't know who you are, you'll allow other things to form your identity. The ramifications of not knowing your identity are major. There are two major issues that come with a lack of identity.

Lack of identity leads to

1. low self-esteem; and
2. low self-efficacy.

A poor self-esteem occurs when we believe we have little value or worth. We see this often when key people in our life are critical toward us, or in our own lives when we are perfectionists, and we see it often when we don't meet our own expectations. There is a second thing that a lack of identity leads to.

Self-efficacy describes how in control of your life you feel. People who have low self-efficacy expectations of themselves will believe they are helpless to influence their fate. For example, when someone says, "I hate my job, but I just can't leave," or "I can't help myself. That's just who I am," it's showing that in this area, there is low self-efficacy. Whenever someone doesn't try to better their life even when they are suffering, it's a sign of low self-efficacy.

Identity is incredibly important. When we attach ourselves to something positive, it impacts how we view ourselves. When we view ourselves in a better light and see results, it leads to confidence and higher self-efficacy.

Grace and Identity

Let's continue reading and see what Paul has to say to us. This next part is crucial in understanding our identity.

> For it is by grace you have been saved, through faith—and this is not from yourselves, it is the gift of God—not by works, so that no one can boast. (Eph. 2:8–9)

Now, this is an important part of the identity puzzle. Often we form our identity in what we do. So if we do what is good, we become prideful. When we mess up, we become shameful. The beauty of grace is that it makes life not fair. We cannot be saved on our own. Way too often, people think about their life through a lens of good versus evil. If we have done enough good, then we hopefully will have outworked our evil and get to heaven. It's a common thought, but it's flawed.

Think about it this way. If someone killed one of your loved ones and then came to you and said, "I'd like to make it up to you. For the next year, I'll make you chocolate chip cookies every Friday." Now, that's fifty-two weeks of cookies versus one sin. How would you feel if that was the offer? You probably wouldn't feel good. Even if the offer was upped to two years or the rest of your life, it may not make a difference. We sin so often we don't even keep track of them. We may remember the big ones, but it's easy to forget the little ones. The times I chose to do what I wanted even though it negatively impacted others was sin. The times I didn't do what I should have done was sin. We don't like to think about our sin. It's sad and can be shameful. Unless we look at our sin through the lens of God's love. God didn't send Jesus to die for perfect people. He sent him to die for sinners in which I am the worst. It's not a competition, but I can sin with the best of them. Thank God for grace. God loves me not because I've been occasionally good but despite the fact that I've royally messed up.

It's impossible to know the love of God if you don't self reflect on your sin. I don't dwell on my sin, but I'm aware of my sin. We don't like to think of our bad choices. We don't like to think of our selfishness, but we won't run to God if we don't understand just how jacked up we are. This isn't to shame us. Remember shame has no place in your life. You have worth because you are God's creation, but you also have some selfishness inside you. Until we wrestle with this, we cannot know the love of God. It's difficult to treat others the way you want to be treated when you haven't come to terms with just how much sin God has forgiven in you. It is by grace we are transformed. That is it is when we realize how jacked up we are then we can start to fathom how loving God is. When we receive the grace of God, it renews us to become new creations. Now, look at what Paul says next. This is the part about identity!

For we are God's handiwork… (Eph. 2:10)

When Paul wrote his letter to the church in Ephesus, he wrote it in Greek. He purposefully chose a word here that we translate to handiwork. The word that Paul used was "poiema," and what he had in mind is a work of masterful creativity. I bet you can already tell this is where we get our English word *poem*. What does that mean for us? Everything! You were not an accident. You are not insignificant. You were created by the master storyteller to be a poem that reflects his greatness. When you know your worth, it changes how you see yourself. In order to get to know your worth, you must get to know the artist.

There are some paintings and sculptures that I think look silly. It doesn't matter what I think. What matters is the price someone is willing to pay for the art. God thinks you are worth paying everything for. So much so that he sent his son Jesus to die for you. Even if no one else around you sees your worth, when you know the artist, you know you have great value. You don't have to compete with others. When you know your worth, you know that others have worth as well. We don't have to put others down to feel good about ourselves. In fact, as a Christian, we never put down other people because in doing so we are insulting God. What if we were secure enough in our identity that we never insulted anyone?

We are God's handiwork or masterpiece, but the verse doesn't stop there. You are God's masterpiece, but let's keep reading.

> For we are God's handiwork, created in Christ Jesus to do good works, which God prepared in advance for us to do. (Eph. 2:10)

You are God's masterpiece created to do good works. What is the good work that you were created to do? That's your purpose. You were created to do good work for God. Your identity is formed by who or what you follow. This is where we get our big idea for this chapter.

Big Idea: When you know who you are, you'll know what to do.

This is why identity is so important. When you know who you are, you will know what to do. When we know who we are, we don't allow others to change us. When we know who we are, we know what decisions to make because it becomes natural for us. In a silly way, it's like this. As a Lakers fan, I know I am not to cheer for the Celtics. Knowing who the Lakers are directs how I see the Celtics. I don't like the Celtics. That's a more negative example. Let me try a more positive one.

While walking through the forest one day, a farmer found a baby eagle who had fallen out of his nest. He looked for the mom and other baby eagles, but they had appeared to have left. He took the baby eagle home to his farm and decided to place it with his chickens. In his mind, this made sense. They are all birds. The chickens were not judgmental and welcomed the baby eagle. Soon, the eagle learned to eat and behave like the chickens.

One day, a naturalist passed by the farm and was blown away with what he saw. He had never seen an eagle act like a chicken. The naturalist asked why it was that the king of all birds should be confined to live in the barnyard with the chickens.

The farmer replied, "Since the eagle has only know the life of a chicken, it had never learned to fly."

From the farmers perspective since the eagle behaved like a chicken, it was no longer an eagle. The naturalist didn't buy that. He declared, "It still has the heart of an eagle and can surely be taught to fly."

The naturalist lifted the eagle toward the sky and said, "You belong to the sky and not to the earth. Stretch forth your wings and fly."

The eagle, however, was confused. He did not know who he was, and seeing the chickens eating their food, he jumped down to be with them again. The naturalist took the bird to the top of the barn and urged him again, saying, "You are an eagle. Stretch forth your wings and fly."

The eagle was afraid of his unknown self and could still see the chickens. Since it was all he had known, he didn't know how to be anything else. The eagle jumped off the man's arm and rejoined the chickens. Finally, the naturalist took the eagle out of the barnyard to a high mountain. He knew he had to get him to a place where he could no longer focus on the chickens.

At the top of the mountain, he held the king of the birds high above him and encouraged him again, saying, "You are an eagle. You belong to the sky. Stretch forth your wings and fly."

The eagle looked around, and then he looked up to the sky. The naturalist lifted the eagle straight toward the sun and the eagle began to tremble. Slowly, he stretched his wings, and with a triumphant cry, soared away into the heavens. The farmer never saw the eagle again. It may be that the eagle still remembers the chickens with nostalgia, but he never returned to lead the life of a chicken.

When a Christian doesn't act like a Christian, it's a sign of an identity issue. When the inner jerk comes out, it's a sign that we've forgotten who we are. When you know you are an eagle, you no longer act like a chicken. When you forget who you are, your actions show it. On the other hand, when you know who you are, you'll know what to do. You are God's masterpiece. When you know who you are, you will know what to do. God created you to fly like an eagle, so stop acting like a chicken. It starts with your identity.

It's Easy to Forget Who We Are

It is so easy to forget who we are and go back to the old way of thinking. You are not a jerk. When you act like one, it's because you've forgotten who you are. Identity is so easily formed that we can take our eyes off Jesus, form our identity in something else, and not even realize it. We need a constant reminder of who we are. That's why to end this book, I want to give you a mantra to repeat. Some of the best leaders in the world use a daily declaration that they read every day. These are statements that remind them who they are. Many great leaders use mantras to draw out their potential. I want to encourage us to do the same thing. If you want to find your identity, find it in Jesus because Jesus doesn't change. Once you know who you are, you will know what to do. It will form your decisions. With that being said, I present the "Kill the Jerk Mantra."

Kill the Jerk Mantra

In Jesus, I am confident. I am disciplined. I am who God says I am. In Jesus, I have everything I need to kill the jerk. Jesus in me is greater than the jerk inside me! I cannot control other people, but in Jesus, I can learn to control myself.

I can seek to understand when I don't agree. I will communicate what is going on inside of me in a healthy way. In Jesus, I have grace. Enough grace to forgive myself. In Jesus, I will treat others like I want to be treated. In Jesus, I will not be passive, passive-aggressive, or aggressive. In Jesus, I will not let pride win. I will ask for help. In Jesus, I will believe the best! I will be intentional and invest in healthy relationships. Through Jesus, I can have healthy relationships! With Jesus's help, I will treat others the way I want to be treated, not how I'm feeling. I can kill the jerk in Jesus's name.

This chapter's Win: View the "Kill the Jerk Mantra" every morning this week. From there, do a second week. Continue doing this until it becomes something you naturally believe. When you forget who you are, come back to this to be reminded of who God created you to be.

Questions for Further Reflection

1. Before reading this chapter how would you answer this question, "Who are you?"
2. What are some things that tempt you to put your identity in them?
3. How would you help someone else find their identity?
4. Based off this chapter, what is God saying to you?
5. What can you do to remember, see, or remind you of the Kill the Jerk Mantra?

KILL THE JERK MANTRA

In Jesus I am confident. I am disciplined. I am who God says I am. In Jesus I have everything I need to kill the jerk. Jesus in me is greater than the jerk inside me! I cannot control other people, but in Jesus I can learn to control myself. I can seek to understand when I don't agree. I will communicate what is going on inside of me in a healthy way. In Jesus I have grace. Enough grace to forgive myself. In Jesus I will treat others like I want to be treated. In Jesus I will not be passive, passive-aggressive, or aggressive. In Jesus I will not let pride win. I will ask for help. In Jesus I will believe the best! I will be intentional and invest in healthy relationships. Through Jesus I can have healthy relationships! With Jesus help I will treat others the way I want to be treated, not how I'm feeling. I can kill the jerk in Jesus's name.

CHOCOLATE CHIP COOKIES

¾ cup sugar
¾ cup brown sugar
2 sticks salted butter (melted)
1 egg
2 ½ cup flour
1 teaspoon baking soda
½ teaspoon salt
12 oz semisweet chocolate chips

1. Heat oven to 375 degrees.
2. Mix both sugars, butter, and egg in a large bowl with a wooden spoon.
3. Stir in flour, baking soda, and salt.
4. Stir in chocolate chips.
5. Drop dough rounded using a scooper or spoon on a cookie sheet or cooking stone.
6. Bake until light brown, eight to ten minutes.
7. Enjoy.

ABOUT THE AUTHOR

Rob Shepherd is the lead pastor of Next Level Church in Yorktown, Virginia. He is the husband to Monica and dad to the Spoofers, Hayden and Reese.

Rob has written two other books, *Even If You Were Perfect Someone Would Crucify You* and *You Misspelled Christian*. His latest book was read by a *New York Times* best-selling author. That's the closest it got to being a best seller. Rob currently has a garage full of this book if you would like a copy.

Pound for pound Rob is the best white pastor who raps. He doesn't do it often, but when he does, he imagines he looks just like TobyMac. Rob wrote this bio himself, so there's that.

One hundred percent of the proceeds of this book go to needy children. Their names are Reese and Hayden. They can be so needy. I kid, I kid.

To connect with Rob find him on social media:
Facebook: Rob Shepherd
Twitter: @robshep
Instagram: rob_shep

CPSIA information can be obtained
at www.ICGtesting.com
Printed in the USA
BVHW022345130220
572250BV00004BA/14